YOU
BELONG

YOU BELONG

A Handbook for Church Members

Revised and Updated

ALLEN H. MARHEINE

THE
PILGRIM
PRESS

Cleveland, Ohio

The Pilgrim Press, Cleveland, Ohio 44115
© 1995 by The Pilgrim Press

Printed in the United States of America on acid-free paper

03   6 5 4

Library of Congress Cataloging-in-Publication Data
Marheine, Allen H., 1931-
You belong : a handbook for church members / Allen H. Marheine. — Rev. ed.
p.   cm.
Includes bibliographical references (p.).
ISBN 0-8298-1104-4 (alk. paper)
1. Church membership. 2. Christian life—United Church of Christ authors.
I.Title.
BV820.M23   1995   95-16991
248.4'85834—dc20   CIP

To Carol,
and to
Louis H. Gunnemann

CONTENTS

PREFACE TO THE REVISED EDITION

FOURTEEN years later! How quickly time passes, and how pleased I am to know that *You Belong* still has life—in an expanded and revised form.

Readers of the original version will note less-specific denominational references. However, they will be aware of this truth: There are often more differences *within* denominations than *between* them. This revision seeks to speak broadly to where most of its readers stand theologically.

The fourteen years have been divided between a chaplaincy directorate and a senior pastor position, with each teaching me well. Many of those lessons have become part of this revision. I thank each for allowing me the privilege of ministry—the Hospital Chaplaincy Council of Miami County (Ohio) and the First United Church of Christ, Troy, Ohio.

I continue to hope that your life is filled with peace and joy in the service of Christ and his church.

PREFACE TO THE FIRST EDITION

ALTHOUGH this book was first envisioned as a brief pep talk piece for a local congregation's Christian enlistment program, it has evolved into a resource for persons joining the church (or for members who want to review the meaning of membership).

No treatment of any subject should be seen as complete. However, I've attempted to provide enough material to whet your appetite. Additional resources are suggested for some of the topics if you wish to pursue them further.

I've included some items that, if presented by your local pastor, could make him or her vulnerable to charges of complaining, begging, looking for sympathy, or being presumptuous. For example, see "Loving Your Pastor." These words need to be said, heard, and lived. The result will be stronger churches and stronger mission.

This manual's present form is far different from the first draft, thanks to many persons, including:

Carol, my partner in marriage and ministry—for her love, insight, and support;

United Church Press, for taking a chance on an unknown author;

Dr. Louis H. Gunnemann (United Theological Seminary of the Twin Cities), the Rev. Victor and Marydel Frohne (St. John's UCC, Bensenville, Illinois), and Dr. Clayton T. Rammler, Southwest Ohio Association Minister, Ohio Conference, United Church of Christ)—reviewers of the first draft, whose comments and encouragement kept this project alive;

St. John's UCC (Germantown, Wisconsin), Pilgrim UCC (Grafton, Wisconsin), St. Paul's UCC (Piqua, Ohio), Peace UCC (Detroit, Michigan)—congregations that have entrusted me with their pulpits and their lives, thereby allowing me the opportunity to serve and to grow;

Rev. Robert Burt, United Church Board for Homeland Ministries, who saw this manual as a resource possibility for use with new members of the church and who made many helpful suggestions;

Terri Henne, my secretary, for typing the manuscript at least twice;

Those who gave permission for quotations to be used.

My hope is that your life in the church will be filled with as much love, meaning, and joy as mine has been. Best wishes to you as a follower of the Christ in your portion of his family.

INTRODUCTION:
FIRST STEP COMPLETED

> *Jesus . . . called to him those whom he wanted . . . to be with him and to be sent out.*
>
> —*Mark 3:13–15*

Congratulations!

You are a member of the Christian church—a living group of persons united by the love of God given through Jesus Christ.

You belong to a *family* that is two thousand years old, with roots again as old.

You belong to a *people* that has had great impact upon the history of the world.

You stand in the great tradition and heritage of those early followers of the Way who "turned the world upside down" (Acts 17:6).

You are a part of a movement—God's—that offers meaning to life and Life to life, dealing not only with present reality but the future as well.

You have a God, a faith, a book.

Congratulations.

And now what?

In the ancient church, following baptism, the new member was given a document—a catechism—pointing out some of the finer aspects of Christian life and practice. One of these early catechisms was the collection of materials now known as the Sermon on the Mount (Matthew 5–7), which deals with the *characteristics* of the Christian life (the Beatitudes), the *impact* of this life (being salt and light), and *how this life works* in daily living.[1]

1

You Belong is for the new (or veteran) church member who wants to be more than just a name on a membership roster. It attempts to answer the question "And now what?" and seeks to be a practical guide dealing with life in a local congregation. *You Belong* follows in the footsteps of other "manuals" of church membership such as the *Didache* (Did-ach-kay), a second-century writing also known as *The Teaching of the Twelve Apostles*.[2]

And now, let's continue our journey.

MORE THAN A BUILDING

> *. . . and to the church in your house.*
> —*Philemon 2*

Chances are your congregation has a meetinghouse, pays utility bills, provides maintenance, and owns some property. Usually a large portion of a congregation's budget is used for the above items, with an equally large portion of time spent on the same in official board meetings.

In all probability, that meetinghouse, the church building, holds a central spot—perhaps too central. This is not to suggest that buildings are unimportant: they provide a service. They are tools for mission. They symbolize the presence of God in the world.

The point to be made is this: *The church is more than a building*. True, you might be asked, "To what church do you belong?" and your answer would probably include reference to some building at a certain address or location. Members of the Church of the Good Shepherd in Ann Arbor, Michigan, refer to their place of worship and activity as a "meetinghouse." (Years ago one's best clothes were identified as "Sunday-go-to-meeting.")

It needs to be remembered that for the first three hundred years of our history, the church was illegal in the eyes of the Roman Empire. Obviously, the church was not prone to have a building on the corner of First and Main, but met (often secretly) in homes, attics, backyards, cemeteries, and other nonpublic locations. Not until 313 C.E. with the Edict of Milan (Edict of Toleration) issued by Emperor Constantine was the church free to come up from "under ground" and meet openly.

The congregation of Pilgrim Church in Grafton, Wisconsin, met in no fewer than three locations (a school lunchroom, a factory office, and a former theater) before the erection of its own meetinghouse. In Grafton, "To what church do you belong?" was answered with, "A group of people, identified as 'Pilgrim,' called together under God, meeting as a family at (one of the three locations) and in the homes of its members to serve God and God's world."

Giving service *to* a building is an ever-present temptation and can become more important than giving service *from* a building. Service to a building often becomes the reason for existence and the chief ministry of the church, as demonstrated by this familiar parable of a lifesaving station, attributed to Canon Theodore Wedel:

> *The lifesaving station [was] built at an especially dangerous spot along the coast. Its only purpose, ostensibly, was to save imperiled lives. It saved a lot of people, but as time went by the saved assumed more and more of the management, and being much more impressed by the beauty of the spot than by the importance of saving lives, they gradually turned the station into an elegant beach club.*[3]

NOT BRICK AND MORTAR,
BUT FLESH AND BLOOD

*To the saints and faithful brothers and sisters in Christ: . . .
we have heard of your faith in Christ Jesus and of the love
that you have for all the saints.*
—Colossians 1:2–4

O n c e past the tendency of equating church with building, the task remains to identify clearly who and what we are. A familiar song states:

> I am the church—
> You are the church—
> We are the church together.[4]

This song reminds us that the church is not a building but is composed of real persons. However, the boy scouts can sing the same song by just changing a word or two—as can the Kiwanis Club, the YWCA, NAACP, AARP, etc. All of these groups can say that they are not a building but a people. So it is that newspaper obituaries list all of the deceased's affiliations including church. The implication drawn from such a listing is that the church is *just* one more organization among many to which one belongs. Wrong!

The author of the biblical book First Peter has a much more comprehensive understanding of the church than its being just one more organization to which we belong.

> But you are a chosen race,
> a royal priesthood,

a holy nation,
God's own people,
in order that you may proclaim the mighty acts of
him
who called you out of darkness into his marvelous
light. (1 Peter 2:9)

A study of this verse will lead you to every other part of the Bible; any biblical commentary will open the broad panorama that is the church. You will discover that WE *are the church* and the *church is Christ's.* And now you face a lifelong adventure in working out in your life what it means to belong to Christ.

The Greek word *laos* (lay-oss) sheds light on the fact of our being the church. From it are derived words such as "laity" and "layperson." This word *laos* means "the *whole* people of God"— all members of the church, ordained and unordained. Unfortunately, the word *laity* has been corrupted and is often misrepresented as "nonprofessional" or "amateur." Hence the ordained (clergy) are the professionals; the unordained (laity or persons in the pews) are the amateurs. This has led to painful separation allowing the professionals to be responsible while the laity become spectators, giving rise to the expression, "Ministers are paid to be good, the rest have to be good for nothing."

"Laos" reminds us that we are the *whole* people of God and, as the hymn "Onward, Christian Soldiers" states it, "all one body, we."

The remainder of this book will, explicitly or implicitly, continue addressing questions such as: Who we are? Why are we?

What is our reason for being, our mission? How do we accomplish that mission?

But always remember, we are a special people, the church, a people unlike any other. We are Christ's own people, we are his!

A MODERN-DAY MIRACLE

> *For just as the body is one and has many members, and all the members of the body, though many, are one body, so it is with Christ.*
>   *—1 Corinthians 12:12 (read all of chapter 12)*

WITH a little imagination supposedly routine Bible passages come alive. For example, note Luke's listing of the twelve disciples (Luke 6:14–16). Among the names are two who make up an interesting combination: Matthew (Levi) the tax collector— unloved by everyone, collaborator with Rome—and Simon the Zealot, a member of that political party dedicated to the overthrow of Roman rule and power. In the same group a traitor and a superpatriot! What interesting times that could produce. But a miracle is in the making; in the presence and work of Christ they become co-workers.

Your congregation is much like those first twelve disciples selected by Jesus. How many differences that come between people are present in your church? There are age gaps and generation gaps; differing political beliefs and parties; vast differences in economic possessions and power; wide differential in education, attitudes, ideas and ideals. There is labor and management. Blue-collar and white-collar workers. Professionals and laborers. All these and more indicate great potential for division. But the miracle of the local congregation is that in spite of the differences, it is a family of God!

Biological families are linked by bloodline, but in a sense we, too, are linked by "blood." (There are many references to the blood of Christ relating to justification, salvation, forgiveness, and, of course, Holy Communion. See 1 Corinthians 10:16–17.)

In spite of personal preferences, likes and dislikes, family feuds and fights and gripes, the local congregation is a reality. It is readily apparent that the church is not made up of perfect people. The classic retort to the complaint of "too many hypocrites in the church" is instructive here: "There is always room for one more."

You are called into the scene of a modern-day miracle. You are invited to know and to love him who makes it all possible: Jesus Christ. You have been called by him into his work, into the people business, into the high calling of making his love a living reality in all the world. And it begins in a tinderbox of possible confrontation—the local church.

We are not a club, for clubs are often composed of like-minded people from the same background. We are a family, a widely differing family, but united with one purpose: being *the family of God in Christ*. The fact that we are together at all is truly a modern-day miracle. Welcome to it!

A later chapter deals with controversy, but suffice it to say here nothing must be allowed to disrupt our unity as a family in Christ.

USING THE REARVIEW MIRROR

> *Long ago God spoke to our ancestors in many and various ways.*
>
> *—Hebrews 1:1*

ROBERT STANGER, the late president of Elmhurst College, while speaking to a youth rally in Madison, Wisconsin, referred to the necessity for church history in terms of an automobile needing a rearview mirror. Dr. Stanger said, "It is important to see where you have been and to see what is following you."

Behind you and alongside you the church is marching through history. Great names. Famous names. And many unsung, anonymous people too. Earth-shattering, life-changing, history-setting events. And you are in that long line. Your name is entered with apostles, evangelists, deacons, popes and kings, women and men, crusaders and missionaries. You stand in storied cathedrals, hot jungles, trackless deserts. You are in freedom marches and in peace demonstrations. You are part of the story of crosses emblazoned on shields and flags raised in the name of Christ on foreign shores.

Seemingly every problem the church could ever face has been faced somewhere in its history. Every heresy has already been exposed. Every challenge has been issued sometime, somewhere, somehow. Now, at this moment, you are part of this rearview mirror. How the church faced life *then* will be instructive as it faces life *now,* as it faces the new but old problems of the day.

You will encounter persons who will say in some form, "I don't need the church; I can be just as good a Christian as those who are members. All I need is to sing my hymns and read my Bible." How sad. And how ignorant. Where did those hymns come from?

9

From where came the Bible? The answers are obvious. They came out of and contributed to the life (history) of the church. Knowledge of this history is to know more about ourselves, and this remarkable story will lead to a deeper appreciation of the drama of salvation in which God has invited us to participate.

You are invited to learn more of your roots, of the story that is now yours. You will discover there is no shortage of materials on this subject.

Additional Resources

Your pastor, the church and public libraries, religious (and secular) bookstores, church school curricula—all are excellent sources for additional information on the history of the church and of your particular portion of it. Three additional suggestions are:

Martin E. Marty, *A Short History of Christianity* (New York: Meridian Books, 1960). Paper, 384 pages. Available from U.S. Catholic Bookstore, 205 West Monroe St., Chicago, IL 60606.

John McManners, ed., *The Oxford Illustrated History of Christianity* (New York: Oxford University Press, 1990). Quite large, a bit expensive, very helpful and interesting.

Friedrich Rest, *Our Christian Symbols* (Cleveland: The Pilgrim Press, 1974).

PART OF THE WHOLE

> *I ask not only on behalf of these, but also on behalf of those who will believe in me through their word, that they may all be one.*
>
> —*John 17:20–21*

In order to belong to the whole, you must become a part. It is possible to be a citizen-at-large of a country, but to enjoy the full privileges of citizenship, a home address is necessary. For example, citizenship in the United States implies the right to vote. However, unless you have a home address, a place of residence, you cannot register, you cannot vote.

So it is with church membership. You don't have the blessings/responsibilities of church membership unless and until you become part of the whole.

It is common knowledge that the church is diverse, with many branches—Russian and Greek Orthodox, Roman Catholic, Protestant. Referring to the latter, there are well over two hundred Protestant churches. Much of this multiplicity has come about through splits, disagreements, even open warfare; some has come about through honest and loving choices to divide; some has come about because of the nature of God (God is so great that no one group could ever completely "cover" every aspect of the grandeur and wonder, the justice and love of God).

Though we despair over our disunity, this is not to suggest that the church is not "ONE." The many parts of the church have been compared to being members of a choir, singing different parts, perhaps even different words, of the same anthem. When that happens, it is a thing of beauty and is worship to

God. (The trouble begins when the "sopranos" will not sit near the "altos" and the "bass" thinks the "tenors" are off-key!)

Though great differences remain theologically between Roman Catholic and Protestant, much of the animosity has disappeared and union and community services are now common in many communities. National and international groups of churches are in existence such as the World Council of Churches (a fellowship of over three hundred churches) and the National Council of the Churches of Christ in the U.S.A. (over thirty communions). In meeting national and international crises many of the churches cooperate.

You have chosen to be a part of the church—you have chosen to be the church. The portion of the church to which you belong has a name. It might be United Church of Christ, or Methodist, or Presbyterian, or Baptist, or Episcopalian, or Brethren, or Nazarene, or Church of God, or—or—or. Regardless of denomination, you are part of the whole. All of the remainder are your brothers and sisters in Christ. The story of your part is also their story—even as their story is yours.

There are many ingredients in the church's mix that point to our being "part of the whole." Aside from many of the great (and minor) names of church history, we share in a rich musical heritage and, of course, we share in the Bible. In addition, there is a common creedal history, with two ancient creeds coming to mind: the Apostles' and the Nicene. Many denominational (and non-denominational) hymnbooks contain one or both forms of these creeds. (A copy of the Apostles' Creed is found in the chapter "What Do We Believe?")

One phrase from the Apostles' Creed has much to suggest to this topic of being a part of the whole. The phrase from the third part reads, "(I believe) the One Holy Universal Christian Church."

Try thinking of the church in terms of "family"—*one* family, with many members. The apostle Paul proves helpful in dealing with our oneness as he writes in Ephesians 4:3–6 about there being "one body, one Spirit, one hope, one Lord, one faith, one baptism, one God and Father of all."

The church is "holy! You are "holy"! Don't let the word hinder you. That which is holy is set aside, designated for a very specific purpose—that purpose is to love, worship, and serve God as modeled and taught by the Savior and Head of the church, Jesus Christ. You being the church—you are designated to love, worship, and serve God.

The church is universal. The earliest versions of the creed used the word *catholic* (small "c"), which means "universal"—we are partners of all who call themselves "church," and we are joined to its history and, as it looks forward, to its future.

And it is Christian—it belongs to Christ. The church is Christ's! Its mission, its task, its purposes are his. When this is forgotten, the church becomes just another organization or club among many. When it is remembered as his, then it (we) becomes the most important work, group, and fellowship of all.

Being the church, being faithful, being the followers of Christ—takes place in a real world of real problems and challenges. The church is not some Mickey Mouse, take-it-or-leave-it activity, it encompasses a life-and-death "Way of Life." And you've chosen to be a part of it.

HAPPY PLOWING

> *No one who puts a hand to the plow and looks back is fit for the kingdom of God.*
>
> —*Luke 9:62*

You've probably seen pictures of old-time plowing: the one furrow plow, Y-shaped, held by the farmer and pulled by a horse or donkey or even a spouse. That kind of plowing was tricky. The plow had to be held at exactly the correct angle or it would dig into the ground or jump out of it. Plowing demanded 100 percent attention at *all* times.

Jesus, in his reference to plowing, suggests that being a member of the church, a Christian, a citizen of the kingdom of God is a 100 percent full-time involvement of time and attention.

He's right.

But that doesn't mean that the Christian Way is a boring and listless way of life. Any Bible reader knows that such was not the case in Jesus' life.

Dietrich Bonhoeffer, a German pastor martyred during World War II, spoke often of the cost and of the joy of discipleship. Several denominational statements of faith refer to the same cost and joy of discipleship. Too often we stress the cost and overlook the joy.

> *Jesus led his disciples in a life not of grim duty but of eager opportunity. He came that [we] might have life and have it abundantly (John 10:10). In the Beatitudes . . . Jesus expresses the joy of the life into which he calls [us] (Matthew 5:3–11). Blessed, he says, are the poor in spirit,*

14

the merciful, the pure in heart. . . . Our English transla-
tion blessed sounds a little more pious than the Greek word
in the New Testament. The writers of the Gospels, report-
ing Jesus' sayings, used one of the two Greek words for
happy—not the ordinary word for happiness, but the word
for exuberant joy.[5]

The New Testament does not describe the church as composed of dull, plodding, unhappy individuals—far from it. Jesus attracted many persons, and he did it not with an unsmiling face. His contemporaries complained about his style, calling him a glutton and a drunkard (Matthew 11:19). These words do not describe an unexciting, boring person.

Christians with long, sad faces are uninformed. They've missed something: the joy of the Gospel. The Greek word *gospel* means good news—and it is ours: the love of God is ours to proclaim, to share, and to live. Can anything as great as God's love leave people untouched and unhappy? The theme of joy is central to the message and mood of the New Testament. One concordance lists at least sixty references to the word *joy* in the New Testament.

This does not suggest that being a follower of Christ is not serious business. It is. But serious business need not be unhappy or unexciting and surely not joyless. Joy is ours in knowing the Christmas and Easter stories; in serving and loving; in reaching out in care and concern; in sharing the good news of God's love; in many forms of ministries to the lonely, aged, ill, lost, young, anxious; in corporate worship; in private prayer, in fellowship with others in the family of Christ.

Happy plowing!

Additional Resource

Dietrich Bonhoeffer, *The Cost of Discipleship* (New York: Macmillan, 1948).

WHAT DO WE BELIEVE?

> *They devoted themselves to the apostles' teaching and fellowship, to the breaking of bread and the prayers.*
> —*Acts 2:42*

IT is anticipated that most persons reading these words will fall into the general category of Protestant—that branch of the church that came into existence during and following the sixteenth-century events called the Reformation that split the Western Church (headquartered in Rome) into two camps: Roman Catholic and Protestant.[6]

We tend to think of "protest" as being negative, against something. The development of the word *Protestant* does have its negative side—applied to both parties of the Reformation.[7]

But it is helpful to examine the positive force of the word and its derivation.

"Pro" means positiveness. One who is *pro* something is *for* something: A pro-American is for America. "Test" is from the Latin root that forms "testify." To testify means to speak the truth as one knows it and believes it. A Protestant, then, is one *who speaks for the truth,* who testifies in a positive way for a particular stand or belief.

We, being Protestant, testify to the following beliefs:

1. Justification by faith
2. The freedom and vocation of the Christian
3. The priesthood of all believers
4. The sufficiency of the Bible[8]

Each of the parts (denominations/groups) of the church has

its particular set of beliefs—often different from others. But most are joined together in more ways than divided. As mentioned earlier, there are often more differences *within* denominations than there are *between* denominations.

For example, though we might not all use formal creeds in our worship services, most of us at one time or another have joined in expressing our common faith using the Apostles' Creed:

> *I believe in God the Father Almighty, Maker of heaven and earth; And in Jesus Christ, his only begotten Son, our Lord: who was conceived by the Holy Spirit, born of the Virgin Mary, suffered under Pontius Pilate, was crucified, dead and buried; he descended into hell; the third day he rose again from the dead; he ascended into heaven and sitteth on the right hand of God the Father Almighty; from thence he shall come to judge the quick and the dead.*
>
> *I believe in the Holy Spirit; the One Holy Universal Christian Church; the communion of saints; the forgiveness of sins; the resurrection of the body; and the life everlasting. Amen.*

Though all of us have great regard for past statements of faith, practically every denomination has made some modern-day declaration of its faith (often mindful and appreciative of others' efforts to do the same). One such declaration as produced by the United Church of Christ follows:

Statement of Faith[9]

> *We believe in you, O God, Eternal Spirit, God of our Savior Jesus Christ and our God, and to your deeds we testify:*

You call the worlds into being,
  create persons in your own image,

and set before each one the ways of life and death.
You seek in holy love to save all people from aimless-
ness and sin.
You judge people and nations by your righteous
    will declared through prophets and apostles.
In Jesus Christ, the man of Nazareth, our crucified
and risen Savior,
    you have come to us
    and shared our common lot,
    conquering sin and death
    and reconciling the world to yourself.
You bestow upon us your Holy Spirit,
    creating and renewing the church of Jesus Christ,
    binding in covenant faithful people of all ages,
        tongues, and races.
You call us into your church
    to accept the cost and joy of discipleship,
    to be your servants in the service of others,
    to proclaim the gospel to all the world
        and resist the powers of evil,
    to share in Christ's baptism and eat at his table,
    to join him in his passion and victory.
You promise to all who trust you
    forgiveness of sins and fullness of grace,
    courage in the struggle for justice and peace,
    your presence in trial and rejoicing,
    and eternal life in your realm which has no end.
Blessing and honor, glory and power be unto you.
Amen.

Most denominations agree in affirming the creativity and love
of God, the Bible as the Word of God, Jesus Christ as Savior, the
sacraments of Baptism and Communion, the church as the fam-

ily of God seeking to be God's servant in the world, and that living the Christian life is an act of thanksgiving to God. And we share in the four classical Protestant beliefs listed earlier:

1. *Justification by faith*: Heaven and eternal life are not ours to earn—they are the gifts of God. This we believe. This is the good news of the gospel—this *is* the gospel. Martin Luther referred to John 3:16 as the *Gospel in Miniature*. God accepts us as we accept God's gift of Jesus Christ. It is in the accepting that we become justified (acceptable) to God.

2. *The freedom and vocation of the Christian*: Among all honorable lines of work, none is better or more God-pleasing than any other. All work is seen as the gift of God—and all work has as its ultimate goal the worship and service of God. The goal is not to be a plumber, or teacher, or nurse, or garbage collector, or home maker—the goal is to be a *Christian* plumber, a *Christian* teacher, a *Christian* nurse, etc.

3. *The priesthood of all believers*: With the tearing of the temple veil in two (Mark 15:38), Protestants believe that access to God is open to all through Christ. We need no other mediator. We appreciate the help we can be to one another to understand this idea and to be comforted and strengthened by one another as we as ministers (priests) love and serve each other. Priests are servants—and we are called to be servants one of the other. Ministry is the privileged work of each member of the family of God.

4. *The sufficiency of the Bible*: Reference to the Bible as being of paramount importance in the life of the church will be made elsewhere in this booklet, as will other aspects of our faith such as baptism and communion. Suffice it to say that all Christians look to the Bible for guidance, for strength, for comfort, for inspiration. Protestants have decided that the Bible is our key and central authority for living life as a

follower of Christ and as his church. It is understated when noted that there are honest and sincere differences in the understanding, interpretation, and use of the Bible. (It must also be said that there are many areas of agreement in the message and purpose of the Bible.)

We are reminded that "beliefs" are more than "intellectual assent to ideas"—beliefs are meant to form the basis for living in a certain way, the Christian way of life. As one Bible verse states, let us not just hear the Word, but let us *do* it as well (James 1:22).

Additional Resources

Martin B. Copenhaver, *To Begin at the Beginning: An Introduction to the Christian Faith* (Cleveland: United Church Press, 1994).

My Confirmation, rev. ed. (Cleveland: United Church Press, 1994). A classic revised. Produced for use by United Church of Christ youth, other denominations will find this a most helpful tool in the training of young people.

Williams R. Myers, ed., *Becoming and Belonging: A Practical Design for Confirmation* (Cleveland: The Pilgrim Press, 1994)

YOUR COURSEBOOK

> *Your word is a lamp to my feet and a light to my path.*
>
> *—Psalm 119:105*

Reverently, she took the box from the top shelf. Blowing away the dust, she opened it. From its cradled resting place the book was lifted. Shining and intact was the gold-embossed date—March 26, 1932. "My confirmation Bible," she announced proudly. "Never been opened. Isn't it beautiful?"

YES, confirmation Bibles are beautiful, but unopened and unused ones are tragedies. Year after year the Bible is listed as a best-seller, but if it is read as little as the above confirmation Bible, it surely is not the best read.

The Christian faith is a faith with a book, the Holy Bible, often referred to as the coursebook of our faith. Actually, the Bible is a collection of books and takes its name from the Greek word *biblos,* meaning library or collection of books.

That which is known as the Old Testament was the Bible of the first-century church. In the span of a few hundred years the New Testament joined it to form the Bible as we know it today. This book, which grew out of and, in turn, spoke *to* the life and mission of the church, conveys the word of God. Through the words, events, and persons of the Bible, God conveys the Word to the followers of Jesus Christ.

The Bible introduces us to God. It is not primarily an *answer book.* Though many persons throughout the history of the church have found in it answers to many of life's perplexing situations,

21

the biblical authors do not indicate their writing as such. Indeed, there is no hint that any of them visualized that their writing someday would become part of a canonical collection called the Bible. (When the New Testament refers to the "scripture," it is thinking of the Old Testament [Jesus' Bible], a collection of books reaching its final form fifty to sixty years *after* the time of Jesus.)

The Bible is a record and an account of God's working among the chosen people—first Israel and then the church—and of how those people responded to God's love and call. The living Christ is made known to us and speaks from its pages. The Bible recounts how the first church members sought to be faithful to Christ, who rose from the dead. Here is found the basis for Christian teaching.

But none of this will be apparent as long as Bibles remain encased in dusty boxes.

As you open your Bible and prepare to enter its world, perhaps the following suggestions will prove helpful.

Enter the Bible as a participant. Become involved. Read it as a participator, not as a spectator. This is your story also, your journey of encountering God.

Don't read it alone. You will, of course, need time for individual reading, but just as the Bible grew out of the life of the church, reading and interpretation of the Bible must take place within that same fellowship. We cannot ignore those who—now and in the past—are (were) engaged in the quest for understanding. Our ideas and conclusions must be open to the scrutiny of others. This is accomplished through group Bible study, the use of guides and commentaries, resource books, correspondence courses, and sermons.

Read many versions. Our age has been blessed with a profusion of versions and translations. Compare them; often a passage that seems obscure in one version will suddenly come alive in another.

Always read with two questions in mind: (1) What did this passage mean to those who first heard it? This will lead you to discover the historical setting, which will help avoid misinterpretation—forcing a verse/passage to say what it never meant to say. (2) What does the passage mean now? Unless Bible study touches the here and now, we are missing the whole point: *The Bible is addressed to real persons in real life.*

Additional Resources

Bernhard W. Anderson, *The Unfolding Drama of the Bible* (New York: Association Press, 1971). An excellent book that quickly traces the story of the Bible in the framework of a play, using acts and scenes.

Diane L. Jacobson and Robert Kysar, *A Beginner's Guide to the Books of the Bible* (Minneapolis: Augsburg, 1991). Provides a concise introduction to each book of the Bible.

Many find the *Daily Study Bible Series* published by Westminster Press suited for both Bible study and devotional reading. The Old Testament is edited by John C. L. Wilson and the New Testament by William Barclay. The series may be bought as a set or as individual volumes.

Other sources for Bible study are *Serendipity, Kerygma,* and *Bethel Series.* Your pastor and/or bookstore will have information about each. Bible study is also available in video form.

YOU'VE BEEN BAPTIZED

> *Go therefore and make disciples of all nations, baptizing them in the name of the Father and of the Son and of the Holy Spirit.*
>
> *—Matthew 28:19*

IN a sermon the Rt. Rev. Chandler W. Sterling, a former Episcopal bishop of Montana, spoke on the function of sponsors in early baptism.

> *You needed at least two baptized Christians, members of the church, to sponsor you. When it came time for your baptism, they would accompany you into the river—one on each side. They would dunk you under—once (in the Name of the Father)—twice (in the Name of the Son)—and a third time (in the Name of the Holy Spirit). Only the third time they held you under, and under, and under. About the time you thought this was the end, they would bring you up.*

Literally, baptism was a matter of life or death. Persons being baptized knew beforehand that they would be held submerged on the third dunking. That's why they selected sponsors they trusted and who loved them. The symbolism is rich: Membership in the church was so important that one's life was laid on the line and was put in the hands of other members.

Baptism is the story of a new life being placed into the fellowship of the church. Baptism also speaks of death—death of a certain way of life in favor of another way; death of rugged individualism ("I can save myself"); death of selfishness and of self-centeredness; death of the "old person" and birth of the "new";

death of commitment to an old community and the entrance into a new people, the church. (See Romans 6:1–14.)

Baptism is bestowing, giving. Some occupations are identifiable by badges—the police, firefighters, various inspectors, pilots, and so on. We have certain expectations of these badges: help and protection from police and fire personnel, ability to fly from a pilot, honesty from inspectors. Baptism bestows a spiritual badge, identifying the wearer as a member of the church. Those who wear the badge of baptism also have expectations placed upon them—love, commitment, generosity, willingness to share and help, worship, certain attitudes.

In this respect note the words of the apostle Paul: "Work out your own salvation with fear and trembling" (Phil. 2:12). At first glance it would seem that he advises self-saving, but not so. We are not corrupting the verse by paraphrasing it, "You have the badge (Baptism) that announces God has saved you; now go, and *live* that baptism."

In a certain part of the United States, baptism of infants is referred to as "having your baby done." Baptism is a once-in-a-lifetime event. The implications of that event will be with us for all time. We've been baptized. We wear the badge that announces we belong to Christ and to his family, the church. Let us live it.

The act of baptizing infants, although not specifically commanded (neither is it specifically forbidden) in the New Testament, places upon the parents, the sponsors, the church, the responsibility to convey to the baptized person the meaning and significance of his or her baptism. The most meaningful way of conveying its meaning *is by living it.*

Churches that practice infant baptism have made provision for that baptized infant at a later time, usually in the early teen years, to publicly confess the Christian faith and to assume more responsibility as a member of the church. In some churches this public ceremony is known as the Rite of Confirmation. The confirmand knows not only the mission of the church but that the church is God's mission in and to the world. It is God who calls, God who selects, God who empowers, God who leads and inspires and acts. It is our task to be available to God who has saved and claimed us. That's what baptism is all about . . . God claiming us for mission, God's mission.

Persons seeking more about Baptism are referred to the 1982 "Faith and Order," Paper No. 111, World Council of Churches, 150 route de Ferney, 1211 Geneva 20, Switzerland. One paragraph, from page 2, is reproduced below:

II. The Meaning of Baptism

2. Baptism is the sign of new life through Jesus Christ. It unites the one baptized with Christ and with his people. The New Testament scriptures and the liturgy of the Church unfold the meaning of Baptism in various images which express the riches of Christ and the gifts of his salvation. These images are sometimes linked with the symbolic uses of water in the Old Testament. Baptism is participation in Christ's death and resurrection (Rom. 6:3–5; Col. 2:12); a washing away of sin (1 Cor. 6:11); a new birth (John 3:5); an enlightenment by Christ (Eph. 5:14); a reclothing in Christ (Gal. 3:27); a renewal by the Spirit (Titus 3:5); the experience of salvation from the flood (1 Peter 3:20–21); an exodus from bondage (1 Cor. 10:1–2) and a liberation into a new humanity in which barriers of division whether of sex or race or social status are transcended (Gal. 3:27–28; 1 Cor. 12:13). The images are many but the reality is one.

Additional Resource

William H. Willimon, *Remember Who You Are: Baptism—A Model for Christian Life* (Nashville: Upper Room, 1980).

YOUR WORK OF MINISTRY

> *The gifts he gave were that some would be apostles, some evangelists, some pastors and teachers, to equip the saints for the work of ministry, for building up the body of Christ.*
>
> *—Ephesians 4:11–12*

YOU know you are a *member* of the church, but did you know you are also a minister? Surprised? Did you think the church hired ordained clergy to do all the work? (Some of the panic felt at the time of a pastoral vacancy often comes from the notion that, without a full-time paid minister, no work is being done.) There is ironic truth in the cliche mentioned earlier, "Ministers are paid to be good; the rest have to be good for nothing." You might not be on the church payroll, but this does not negate the fact you are a minister.

You wear the badge of baptism, which identifies you as a minister, one called upon to work. Work is not limited to the professional.

Another version of the Bible translates the latter part of the above verse from Ephesians as: "He did this to prepare all God's people for the work of Christian service" (TEV).

Did you catch it? *All God's people!* That's you, that's me. To emphasize this point, one congregation includes, along with listing the names of the pastoral staff in its Sunday worship bulletin, a line, "Ministers: All the Members."

Recall the discussion in the chapter "What Do We Believe?" and the reference there to the vocation of the Christian and the priesthood of all believers.

Because none of us are exactly the same and each of us has

various and differing gifts, your ministry will be special and unique. You might not preach on Sunday (though some churches allow/encourage lay messages); you might not lead in worship (some congregations enjoy lay liturgists); but you will be involved in meaningful ministry.

Perhaps a definition of "ministry" is in order:

> *Ministry is any act of word and/or deed that is performed for the glory of God, in response to God's love, in which persons are loved and served and in which God is honored and the church is enhanced.*

Your ministry might be one of music or education; it might be one of cooking or sewing; maybe it is visiting or administration. Your ministry is not confined to a particular place or time—but as a Christian, a member of the church, you are always "on duty" loving, serving, helping, learning—to the glory of God! Even those who are confined to home or hospital can engage in a ministry of prayer for others and be sources of love and sunshine for those who enter their world.

You were called into the family of the church, not to loaf, but to lift; not to watch, but to work; not to sleep, but to serve. May yours be an effective ministry.

What is being discussed is the relevance or irrelevance of the church. May the following anecdote, first heard during an Ohio pastors' convocation, never apply to you!

> *Did you hear about the pastor who fell asleep while preaching? The congregation didn't notice: they were already sleeping. And they all slept 'til Tuesday—and nobody missed them!*

MEANING OF WORSHIP

> *I was glad when they said to me, "Let us go to the house of the Lord!"*
>
> —*Psalm 122:1*
>
> *O come, let us worship and bow down, let us kneel before the Lord, our Maker!*
>
> —*Psalm 95:6*

Sunday morning, 7:30 A.M.
zzzzzzzzzzzzzzzzzzzzzzzzzzzzzzzzz
Rrrrrrriiiiiinnnnnnnngggggggggg
Click! Ahhh, bed feels sooo goood!
zzzzzzzzzzzzzzzzzzzzzzzzzzzzzzzzz

or

Sunday morning, 7:30 A.M.
Time to get moving—
tee off at eight,
grass needs cutting,
laundry to do,
shopping to be done.

or

Sunday morning, 7:30 A.M.
zzzzzzzzzzzzzzzzzzzzzzzzzzzzzzzzz
Rrrrrrriiiiiinnnnggggg—Click!
Time to get up! Time for church!

Why go to church? Why worship? Why leave that warm bed? Why not practice my chip shot? Why worship? Because you promised you would. When you joined the church you promised to

29

worship regularly. Not now and then, but regularly. Not when the weather was right or when you felt like it. Not when you had nothing else to do. But regularly.

Imagine someone saying, "I want to belong to my neighborhood association, but I'm not going to attend any meetings." Or, "I want to be a Mason or to join my professional organization or be part of a fraternity/sorority, but don't ask me to become involved in anything the group does, and of course I will be absent when the group meets." Ridiculous. But too often this is the case when it comes to church members and worship.

Perhaps we need to sharpen our definition of worship or, better, first decide *what worship is not*. It is not a show performed by the choir, the organist, and the minister in which the offering is the price of admission. It is not a ritual performance guaranteed to bring good luck or to secure favor from some deity. ("God, I've been a good person. See, I've come to your church. Now, you be good to me, okay?") Worship is more than a voluntary gathering of a club called the church, and it surely is not a social event for the purpose of displaying a new wardrobe.

If the above defines what worship is not, what is it?

One definition of worship is that "it is the celebration of the presence of God." Another: "Worship is our response to God's love and gifts." Still others: "Worship is the work of the church." "Worship is our response to the experience of encountering God on God's terms."

The first nine verses of Isaiah 6 are helpful for an understanding of worship. In highly symbolic language Isaiah describes how he was called into the ministry, how he became a prophet. But we find a bonus: a moving experience of worship and a vivid listing of the elements (or steps) of worship.

> 6:1–4 Praising God; knowing the might and power
> of God.

6:5 After "seeing" God one is forced to "see" self. The result is confession of sin and recognition of life as it is.

6:6–7 The worshiper is aware of God's love and forgiveness. There is hope for the human situation.

6:8a In worship, God speaks.

6:8b In worship, we respond, "Here am I, Lord! Send me."

And Isaiah went to work! (The order of worship is often referred to as the *liturgy,* which derives from an ancient word meaning "the work of the people.")

You will find, in your church's order of worship, all the above elements. You might even find them in the above order; but regardless of order, these ingredients of worship are present. In any event, the church needs to worship to live. Take away the worship service of the church and soon there will be nothing left. This has already been acknowledged by the author of Hebrews as nonworshipers are addressed. (See Hebrews 10:25.)

The importance of regular worship to the life of the church can be compared to the burning coals of fire. When they are together they put out their combined heat. Separate one coal from the rest and watch that coal slowly cool and become gray, cold ash.

To this point what has been said concerning worship could be generally applied to other faiths—surely to the Jewish faith and to the faith of Islam. What differentiates these from Christian worship? One word—or two—Jesus Christ!

We worship "in the name of Jesus Christ." In worship we are confronted by his word; we are members of his church; we pray in his name; we have set aside as a special day of worship the Day of Resurrection; we bear witness to him as the Savior and the Son of God, just as the first-century followers did. With Paul we exclaim, "We preach Christ crucified" (1 Cor. 1:23). The central act of worship revolves around his "breaking the bread . . . and giving the cup." Worship takes place within a fellowship of persons who bear his name, *Christ-ian* (those belonging to Christ).

In great thanksgiving for the blessing of God, as made known and given through God's child, we worship. Without this thanksgiving there is no worship.

So come, join the fellowship. Come and worship. You've got the greatest reason in the world—there, in worship, is One who has died for you, who will meet you, speak with you, send you out into God's world and mission.

Additional Resources

Imaging the Word: An Arts and Lectionary Resource, volume one (Cleveland: United Church Press, 1994). A primary resource book for the "Word Among Us" curriculum. Background for the lectionary used in many churches each Sunday. This is the first of three volumes tracing the movement of the three-year lectionary cycle.

James F. White, *Introduction to Christian Worship,* rev. ed. (Nashville: Abingdon, 1990). A survey of worship through the ages; the meaning behind our liturgical practices.

GREAT SERMONS NEED
GREAT LISTENERS

> For Christ did not send me to baptize but to proclaim the
> gospel, and not with eloquent wisdom, so that the cross of
> Christ might not be emptied of its power. For the message
> about the cross . . . is the power of God.
> —1 Corinthians 1:17–18

*Bemoaning the lack of great pulpit names and
pulpiteers, the old-timer sighed, "Ah, there were great
preachers back then." "Yes," agreed his younger compan-
ion, "and there were great listeners back then."[10]*

Assume that you'll be an active member for fifty years and
that you will hear fifty sermons a year. That's twenty-five hundred sermons and, if they average twenty minutes in length, that's
833 hours or five full weeks of nonstop sermon listening!

Preaching has been with the church from its beginning. There
is no indication that preaching will not remain with the church,
indeed not continue to be a major part of the worship service.

Most church historians agree that preaching has never been on
as high a plain as now. Generally, preachers are better prepared
and are more skilled than in any period of the church's life. True,
there is an absence of the awe and attention accorded some of the
church's "pulpit princes" of past generations, but general level of
excellence has risen throughout the church.

How can *you* become a great listener? (And it has even been
suggested that great listeners draw forth great sermons.) Here are
some hints on becoming a great listener.

1. *Come to worship.* Unless worship is your purpose for coming, even the greatest sermons by the best preachers will make little impact upon you.

2. *Pray for the preacher.* Ask God's help for the one who is bringing the message. (It is difficult to think negative thoughts regarding one for whom you are praying.)

3. *Pray for yourself and your fellow worshipers.* Seek God's help for alertness, attentiveness, and for wisdom and ability to apply the message to the life situation.

4. *Anticipate.* Think on the title, scripture text, and service theme. Anticipate the content and direction of the message. Expect some "fire"!

> *The visiting preacher was about to begin the sermon. He glanced at the pulpit floor, stooped suddenly, and arose holding the fire extinguisher which was always stored there. Holding it aloft he declared, "The last place you want a fire extinguisher is in the pulpit!"*

5. *Participate.* Be alert, sit up, don't slump. Don't relax, for the mind will follow the body's lead. Maintain eye contact with the preacher. Physically or mentally jot down key words, ideas, points. Relate the sermon to your situation—not to "so-and-so" who should have been here to hear this."

Reflect upon these words of Paul: "So faith comes from what is heard, and what is heard comes through the word of Christ" (Romans 10:17). Expect to be confronted. The sermon is not just for those who didn't show, it is for you; just as the prayers, the anthem, and the scripture reading are. The preacher is not "aiming" at you; the Word of God is at work here. Look for it. Expect it.

6. *Follow up.* Share your reactions, agreement, suggestions, and,

yes, even disagreements with the preacher. What will be different in your life because of this sermon?

7. *Remember that God is able, through the "foolishness of preaching," to make the Way known to us, God's people.* (See 1 Corinthians 1:17–2:5.)

8. Finally, by emphasizing twenty minutes of the customary sixty-minute worship service, *we are not downgrading the total worship experience* or the great significance of God's people gathered together. (See the previous chapter, "Meaning of Worship.")

P.S.: "Be doers of the word, and not merely hearers" (Jas. 1:22).

Additional Resources

Church and pastors' libraries and most bookstores have an abundance of sermon collections on almost any topic. Examples of effective children's sermons can be found in the works of Jerry Marshall Brown published by The Pilgrim Press, Cleveland. Titles include: *The Brown Bag: A Bag Full of Sermons for Children, Another Brown Bag,* and *One More Brown Bag.*

EAT . . . DRINK . . .
IN REMEMBRANCE OF HIM

> *Take, this is my body . . . this is my blood of the covenant.*
> *—Mark 14:22–25*

The pastor had just begun preaching when Mrs. Rennicke jumped from her seat and rushed out the door. "Hmmm," assumed the pastor, "she's not feeling well." But before the conclusion of the sermon she returned. "Good," thought the pastor, "she's feeling better." Greeting worshipers at the door following the service he inquired of Mrs. Rennicke as to her health. "Oh, that!" she laughed, "I remembered I forgot to put the water on the potatoes!"

THERE are different forms of remembering. Recall is one. Our minds are busy at this task all the time, bringing to consciousness bits and pieces of information—some of importance, some trivial: the score of last night's game, a telephone number, the name of a forgotten friend, an historical event. In its own quiet way this form of remembering goes on continually. Then there is the kind of remembering—like Mrs. Rennicke's—that *leads to action!* It is this kind of remembering Jesus had in mind when, taking the bread and the cup in that upper room, he said, "Do this in remembrance of me."

How important to the life of the church and to your life is the sacrament of Holy Communion? (This sacrament is known by many titles: Lord's Supper, Lord's Table, Holy Eucharist, Agape Meal, Love Feast, Sacrament of the Upper Room.) One traditional order of worship refers to the celebration of Holy Communion as "the innermost sanctuary of the whole Christian Worship."[11] Holy Communion was so central to the life of the church that the word coined to indicate someone removed from the fellowship of the church was *excommunication*—literally, "out of communion."

Holy Communion is important because of whom we remember and what this remembering leads to.

In this sacrament we remember the head of the church, Jesus the Christ, and his gifts to us. We see again the drama of God reconciling the world to the Godself. We are conscious of a new covenant of love and grace founded upon the one who calls us to remember him. We are mindful of one another and discover (remember) that we are one family, a family eating together.

This author's childhood family was as active as most—seldom together at any given time. But mom and dad had one rule: "On Sunday noon, we all eat together." (At least once a week we bore witness to our being a family!)

In the celebration of Holy Communion we remember words of faith, of commitment, and we thank God for the facts of forgiveness and strength conveyed through the action of the Holy Spirit.

Notice the use of the word *celebration*. Holy Communion is an act of celebration. We celebrate the risen Lord and his victory over sin, death, and the grave. We celebrate Christ's call to us to join him in the family of God, the church. We remember, we celebrate, we live as Christ's followers.

To some persons a word such as celebration appears out of place. They remember the somber, almost sad atmosphere of the communion service. Celebrations generally revolve around those persons and events for which we are thankful. In Holy Communion—and here is meant the total experience, all that is said and done and felt—there are many reasons for giving thanks. As mentioned earlier, some fellowships use the word *eucharist* to identify the sacrament. The word means *thanksgiving* and was the title of the Prayer of Thanksgiving found in the traditional service of communion. We give thanks that Jesus Christ, our Savior, lives. We rejoice that he is present and active in his church. We celebrate that in the symbolism of the bread and wine/grape juice, we meet the living Christ, active in and among us. We seek to follow the exhortation of the apostle Paul when he speaks of proclaiming Christ! (See 1 Corinthians 11:26.)

How often should you take communion? (Many prefer "celebrate" to "take.") The answer to this question lies in how often you need to be reminded of who you are and of what Jesus has done. Is there significance in the fact that the ancient church communed in each service? In the Protestant portion of the church there appears to be a trend toward increasing the frequency of celebrating the sacrament. Some congregations commune each time they gather to worship.

A topic of great interest in some congregations concerns children and their participation in communion. Some fellowships look upon communion as a "privilege" earned following the successful completion of a course of study (Confirmation). Others, seeking to include children in the full life of the church, think of communion more as a "family meal" in which all participate. Some churches suggest age limitations (e.g., third grade and above). Some allow parents or guardians to determine the extent of their child's participation. In any scenario, it is assumed that an educational effort is underway to help children understand communion.

An ancient liturgy called for the "Feeding of the Five Thousand" (Mark 6:30–51) to be read during the service of communion. This passage portrays the disciples, at the conclusion of the meal, being commanded by Jesus to enter a boat. Later, in great distress (a storm), they are met and saved by Jesus. Symbolically, we see the church in worship (communion) and then being sent out into the world (sea) where it not only meets difficulty (storm) but its Lord as well and remembers him. Holy Communion is not an escape from the world. Rather, it is a service of remembering him who sends us out into the world for which he lived and died.

Note the relationship between baptism and communion; communion is a time of remembering our baptism and all of its meanings. We look back to the event wherein we became the church; we look forward to an ever-deepening commitment of being the faithful church.

Additional Resource

Material on communion may be found in "Faith and Order," Paper No. 111, World Council of Churches, Geneva, Switzerland.

HOW MUCH SHALL I GIVE?

> *They gave themselves first to the Lord.*
> —*2 Corinthians 8:5*

"Reverend," the potential member asked, "does your church pledge? Because if it does, I'm not going to join. I just don't believe in pledging." (That church did—and he didn't.)

Of course, when you joined the church you knew that there would be a financial cost involved. The question is not if I give, but rather how much to give and in what spirit?

Strange how the word *pledge* drives people away. Isn't it odd that persons with twenty-year mortgages on their homes, three years of payments on their autos, buying furniture on time, and taking out loans for their children's college education will refuse to commit themselves to a year's giving to their church?

It just does not seem consistent, does it? Are those who refuse to join or pledge saying that houses, cars, furniture, and education are important and that their church support is not?

What is a pledge? Simply a written or oral statement of intention. Some congregations use words other than pledge—Declaration of Intent; Estimate of Giving; My Love Gift. Call it what you will, it indicates that you have come to grips with the meaning of Christian stewardship and with what it means to be a part of Christ's work and mission in the world:

The English word steward *is derived from the Middle English* stigweard *or* styward. *A styward was one who kept the pigpen in the summer so that the household would not starve in the winter. Styward became steward, which signified one who cared for the livelihood and survival of the household.*[12]

A steward is one given responsibility. The most common use of the word is found in the airline industry where such a person is given the responsibility to care for a planeload of people. This responsibility is seen as the "gift" of the airline to the steward. (If the "gift" is not given, it means that one is unemployed and is in trouble.)

The creation stories in Genesis 1 and 2 announce the gifts of God to us—and that we are also God's creation. We are challenged to receive and to use these gifts gladly, thankfully, responsibly.

The size of our gift, in proportion to our resources, indicates how seriously we consider ourselves God's and how thankfully we have accepted God's *gifts* (and whether we think of what we have as gifts at all).

One ideal is proportionate giving—giving a definite and significant proportion of your income. (See 2 Corinthians 8:8–15; 9:6–15.)

Another biblical model for giving is the tithe—10 percent. Many references are made to this practice, both in and out of the Bible. But legalism is to be avoided. Giving needs to be significant, enjoyable, life-changing.

The "fair share plan" does not apply to churches. Under this plan the amount of money needed is divided by the number of givers, and the answer is your "fair share." Actually, we do not give to a church budget—we give to our Risen Savior and his work through his church. The practice of Christian stewardship is not based upon the need of the church to receive; rather it is based upon the need of the Christian to give.

A man about to be baptized in the lake tossed his wallet to his wife to keep it safe and dry. The pastor intercepted the toss and handed it back with the words, "Your wallet, too, needs to be baptized!"

Of course, there are other related forms of giving of our time and abilities, our love and caring.

Question 1: What is your only comfort, in life and in death?

That I belong—body and soul, in life and in death—not to myself but to my faithful Savior, Jesus Christ, who . . . makes me wholeheartedly willing and ready from now on to live for him.[13]

Baptism and stewardship are closely linked; in fact, they are inseparable. Baptism declares that we belong, not to ourselves, but to Christ whose name we bear (Christian). And not only ourselves, but all we are and own. Baptism declares that Christ is to be central in our decision as to how we use the gifts of God. (It is apparent that stewardship involves much more than dividing a budget by total members to fix an average.)

Personalize your giving, it is you! It is you giving not to a piece of paper called a budget but you going to persons, to causes, to ministries, to challenges and opportunities, to the work of God's love, to the mission of God in the world.

Just a thought about moneymaking projects. As defined, the concept of Christian stewardship is based upon God's gimmick-free gift of love to each of us. Can our response be in the same spirit? Gimmick-free! Moneymaking projects can monopolize the time and energy so desperately needed in the church's mission. The following quote, source unknown, deserves some reflection: "Jesus sent us into the world, but not to sell Christmas cards; and he said, 'Feed my sheep—but not at $6 a head.'"

LOVING YOUR PASTOR

> *This is my commandment, that you love one another as I have loved you.*
>
> *—John 15:12*

YOU *are* a minister and each congregation has as many ministers as it has members.

One or more of these may be an *ordained* minister. One definition of ordination is:

> *In ordination the church sets apart, by prayer and the laying on of hands, those of its members whom God has called to serve . . . as pastors and teachers within the mutual ministry of all believers. They are to preach [God's] Word, to administer the sacraments, to prepare the church for its witness in the world, to be instruments of healing in the lives of [all], and to guide the community of believers in its common work.*[14]

God's commandment calls for love: "Love one another." This section calls for you to work diligently at loving your pastor. Naturally, you expect your pastor to love you. Can your pastor expect the same?

Part of loving is understanding. When you understand the tension, the calling, the working of the ordained pastoral office, you'll be in a better position to minister and to love.

> *"It is a lonely, scary feeling," confided the pastor to a friend. "My congregation looks so healthy, but actually, spiritually speaking, we're dead! I felt driven to do some-*

thing; and I did, Sunday, in the Sermon. I asked them to come with me on a journey, a journey that is still unclear. But we've got to do something. We're so dead. I'm scared. I don't know what I'll do if some don't come along."

This frightened pastor is not an exception; he's more like the rule. He feels compelled to lead, but in this day and age of "democracy" shouldn't one first appoint a committee, do a study, seek congregational approval? Many pastors find themselves between the demands of the gospel to proclaim the Word as it is urgently unfolding in their lives and a general expectation of not to "rock the boat" or a concern for peace, quiet, and public relations. An officer of a congregation said to the new pastor: "Reverend, we're glad you're our new preacher. But I just want you to know that we don't talk about three things—beer, money, and labor problems." (Can you guess what the sermon topics were in that church the next three Sundays?)

The Rev. Ernest T. Campbell, former senior minister of the Riverside Church in New York City, makes it quite clear that pastors who are called to serve Christ in all humility are also to lead the church in all strength and courage.[15] This can lead to that same dilemma experienced by the prophet Jeremiah:

If I say, "I will not mention him, or speak any more in his name," then within me there is something like a burning fire shut up in my bones; I am weary with holding it in, and I cannot. (Jeremiah 20:9)

Jesus was never accused of not leading. (Some of the disciples did wonder, however, about *where* they were being led.) Jesus' leadership style was one of service; picture him in the upper room washing and toweling the feet of his disciples. (The stole, at times compared to the "yoke" of service given by Jesus, is linked also to this towel of Jesus.[16])

It is a difficult tightrope to walk, this rope of expectation that each member has for the pastor. One of the greatest acts of love between pastor and congregation is to understand together, with the style of Jesus in mind, the leadership of the pastor.

By "love" is meant God's love; John 3:16 kind-of-love; 1 Corinthians 13 kind-of-love (love is patient, kind, not arrogant, not rude, not resentful, not pushy).

Remember that your pastor is uniquely equipped to minister. Encourage and enable this to happen. By so doing, the love of Christ will be brought to bear. What an awesome, privileged, scary task to be entrusted with the soul(s) of a congregation!

But those who bring the love of Christ are also human and are subject to the same sins, temptations, fits of anger, periods of depression as are all members of the church. They stand in need of forgiveness, grace, and ministering as much as anyone. A pastor does not stand above the congregation but with it. Pastors can be angry, upset, disappointed, frustrated, thereby requiring the ministry of understanding and the love you have to offer.

Love and trust are closely related. To love your pastor means to entrust her or him with your life, your problems, your cares. To love is to allow your pastor to have the same problems. Knowing this you will not be inclined to criticize too quickly.

We expect pastors to minister to us in our needs. Who pastors the pastor? Who ministers to the minister? We expect pastors to pray with us. Who prays for the pastor? We expect the pastor to love. Who loves the pastor. You can.

Some specific things you can do: (1) Share your love through volunteering for work, through understanding, face-to-face. (2) Provide time for the pastor's self-renewal (money too) and give enough provision for the pastor's family responsibilities. (Although pastors are on call twenty-four hours a day, they are not expected to work twenty-four hours a day!)

Love your pastor—the effort will be worth it and the result will amaze you. If you must disagree or criticize, do it personally, face-to-face, seeking the best for Christ's church.

Additional Resource

Robert G. Kemper, *What Every Church Member Should Know About Clergy* (Cleveland: The Pilgrim Press, 1985).

WHEN ASKED TO SERVE

> *Then I heard the voice of the Lord saying, "Whom shall I send, and who will go for us?" And I said, "Here am I; send me!"*
>
> *—Isaiah 6:8*

As a member of a congregation, it is likely that you will be asked to assume responsibility: sing in the choir, teach in the church school, do telephoning, usher, greet worshipers, serve on the official board, be a friendly visitor—there are any number of opportunities to serve.

It will probably be another member or the pastor who asks. You might be tempted to treat the request as insignificant. You might refuse. You might present excuses why you must decline. If so, you stand in distinguished company; even Moses tried (unsuccessfully) to refuse God's call. (See Exodus 3–4.)

A sentence appearing in an installation service for church officers is quite enlightening:

> *Although your election has been by . . . your fellow members, you are not to regard yourselves merely as servants of [human beings], but also as servants of Christ.*[17]

Even though the invitation to serve comes through persons, it comes, first, from Christ, the Head and Ruler of the church. When this fact is accepted, can anyone say no?

> *One pastor, addressing our inclination to say "no" to the church and its needs, while we find time and energy for everything else, suggested in a sermon that we take our*

excuses and alibis to Christ—"Just lean a ladder against the cross, climb it, look Jesus right in the eyes, and then give him your excuses."

Those who consider the church to be just another club, social organization, volunteer group (one among many to which they belong), or some humanitarian venture, such as the Red Cross or the American Cancer Society will find it rather easy to say no to requests that involve them personally. But those who consider the church as God's instrument of love and peace—as God's mission in the world—will find it difficult to be negative. Rather, they will know it to be an honor and a privilege to be invited by God to serve in God's world as God's messenger and example of love.

The same service of installation quoted earlier continues:

> *It is a great honor to bear office in the Lord's house, so is it also a solemn trust which no one should take upon him/herself rashly or lightly. Magnify your office and make high account of its duties as a service to be rendered unto God.*

With so much to be done and for so grand a heavenly Parent and so great a Lord as ours, why wait to be asked? There are more opportunities for service than persons to fill them.

Happy Serving!

MEETINGS—MEETINGS—MEETINGS

> *The apostles and the elders met together to consider this matter.*
>
> —*Acts 15:6*

As an active, participating member of your congregation, you will not be able to avoid going to meetings. We trust that your meetings will have more content than the one written about by an anonymous poet:

> We have met,
> And we have et;
> If we hadn't et,
> We wouldn't have met.

Nothing dampens enthusiasm and kills spirit more quickly than a dull, going-nowhere meeting. To help avoid that possibility, you might apply the suggestions listed below to meetings in which you participate.

Know the purpose of the meeting. A meeting with no stated purpose will wander aimlessly and waste time.

Set an agenda. Determine what needs to be done. Know what needs to be accomplished in the meeting.

Be on time; finish at a set time. Courtesy demands the prompt beginning of a meeting at the stated time. Waiting for latecomers is disrespectful to those who were on time. Being late is discourteous. Setting a definite ending time helps to keep discussion moving and centered on the agenda and purpose.

Participate in the meeting. Do your homework, your preparation. Listen. Contribute. Don't be content with allowing others to do your share.

Be sensitive to the "hidden" agendas. We all bring hopes, frustrations, expectations, axes to grind. Much of the "other" business will become evident. Allow time or make time to deal with *all* the business.

Remember the purpose of the church. It is surprising, even frightening, how much so-called church work has nothing to do with the work of the church. We are a special people; our meetings will bear witness to what we are. *And what we are is the church of Jesus Christ.*

Additional Resource

Philip A. Anderson, *Church Meetings That Matter* (New York: The Pilgrim Press, 1987).

ANNUAL MEETINGS:
BANE OR BLESSING?

> *Then Joshua gathered all the people . . . and recounted all God had done . . . and then challenged them . . . "Choose this day whom you will serve."*
>
> —*Joshua 24:1, 15*

Almost all congregations gather at least once a year for that business meeting known as the annual meeting. Your congregation is probably no exception. The meeting is held for the purpose of elections, hearing of reports, acting upon budgets, and discussing various items of business.

Stereotyped badly, the approach of the annual meeting is not signaled by cheers of joy. More often than not, there is an attitude of deep resignation to the inevitable: "Let's get it over with."

Yet annual meetings come from a distinguished past, including that of the people of Israel, who heard Joshua challenge, "I know not what others will do, but as for me and my house, we will serve the Lord." Then there were the Jerusalem conferences, which saw important decisions made and dedicated persons chosen to serve God. (See Acts 15.)

Annual meetings can be a bane or a blessing in the life of a congregation. They will be blessings when each member takes personal responsibility in being present and participating. (This is the locale for the church's work, not in grumbling groups in the church parking lot or in the local pub afterward.)

Your meeting will be meaningful, productive, and significant—not a waste of time—if the following principles are followed:

1. Be aware of the contents of the chapter "When Controversy Erupts."
2. See the meeting as needing the participation of *all* the membership. When the 10 percent who are present speak for the absent 90 percent, trouble lies ahead.
3. Set new goals and evaluate those established earlier. Be reasonable, yet courageous, in your goal setting. Be specific, so that proper evaluation can be made later. For example, rather than setting as a goal "We are going to work harder on evangelism this year," state it more precisely: "This year our evangelism committee will train five teams of two persons each to make a total of fifty calls to add least twenty new members."
4. Share cares and concerns relating to the total membership (including how to involve more persons in the annual meeting).
5. Insist on careful planning. Mail materials beforehand so that participants will be well informed and ready to discuss the issues at hand intelligently.
6. Celebrate the highlights of the past year.

The one continuing item on the agenda—"Thy will be done"—is based on Matthew 6:10. What would God have us be and do? The annual meeting is an appropriate place for this question. It is so important an item that none should take lightly the responsibility/opportunity of the annual meeting.

LET ME PRAY!

> *He was praying in a certain place, and after he had finished, one of his disciples said to him, "Lord, teach us to pray."*
>
> —*Luke 11:1*

Hᴏᴡ's that? Shouldn't it be, "Let *us* pray"? Must be a mistake. No mistake, and nothing to fear. Why shouldn't *you* be able to pray? You believe in God, right? Hence, you can speak with God.

Many members of the church have convinced themselves that unless a prayer sounds like it has come from three years of seminary training and twenty years of pastoral experience, it is not adequate. ("Oh, Reverend, *you* pray. When you pray it sounds so much like a prayer.")

> *Jesus' counsel would be: "When you are praying, do not heap up empty phrases as the Gentiles do; for they think that they will be heard because of their many words."*
> *(Matthew 6:7)*

Who claims prayer is the privilege of the clergy? Who says only pastors can pray in public? (Clergy are often pleased when *not* asked to lead in prayer.)

There will probably come a time when you will be asked to lead a group in prayer. Of course, you have your personal prayer life, but in public? "Oh, no! I can't!" you say. But you can.

Your prayer need not be long, need not be fancy, need not be complicated. God will hear you. There are no unlisted numbers or private lines when it comes to prayer. Pray what needs to be prayed. No less, no more.

53

For variety, besides using spoken prayer, you could ask the group to begin with silent prayer, each person asking God's help and blessing for the work at hand.

Another type of prayer is the "bidding" prayer. Begin with a brief statement such as, "Let us thank God for our congregation." (Brief period of silent prayer.) Then, "Let us seek God's help for this meeting." (Silent prayer.) "Let us pray for one another." (Silent prayer.) And so on. Nothing extravagant, but meaningful and sincere.

You can create a well-rounded prayer by patterning it after the content and style of the Lord's Prayer—or you could resort to a familiar memory device, using the letters in the word "acts." A "complete" prayer contains these elements:

> A—God is *A*dored, praised, worshiped, glorified.
>
> C—Faith in God is *C*onfessed, as is sin *C*onfessed.
>
> T—*T*hanksgiving for the gifts of God.
>
> S—Make known *S*eekings, *S*upplications—your askings.

This last type of prayer (S) includes "intercessory"—asking God to intervene in some situation either for us or someone else. It is one of the most troublesome and perplexing prayers for many persons.

An excellent resource to help is *The Workbook of Intercessory Prayer,* by Maxie Dunnam. First published in 1977 by the Upper Room, Nashville, it is in its eighth printing.

If you have advance notice, examine some of the books that are available in your church library or local bookstore. In addition, many hymnals have excellent resource sections. There is great challenge and satisfaction, however, in writing your own.

Additional Resources

John Baillie, *A Diary of Private Prayer* (New York: Scribner, 1949). A classic—30 days of morning and evening prayers.

Maxie Dunnam, *The Workbook of Living Prayer*, rev. ed. (Nashville: Upper Room, 1994). Learning to pray in a simple, practical way.

DEVELOPING A SPIRITUAL LIFE

> *The fruit of the Spirit is love, joy, peace, patience, kindness, generosity, faithfulness, gentleness, and self-control.*
> —*Ephesians 5:22*

THE title of this chapter may be misleading.

Those who are into organizational flow-charts might see the progression in these steps: (1) I become acquainted with the Christian way of life and the church; (2) I decide to join the church; (3) As a member of the church I desire to become more spiritual; (4) I take steps to develop a spiritual life.

When asked what the spiritual life looks like, the usual answer includes instruction about taking time on a regular basis to read the Bible, to pray, to meditate. In other words, "regular personal devotions"—a daily five to ten minutes with God.

Then, following our fragmentary way of dividing and organizing life, that time is called my "spiritual life."

Although you are urged to develop a personal worship and prayer time, remember that spiritual life encompasses *all* of life. The spiritual life is a life in touch with and attuned to God. The spiritual life is one that knows God in all circumstances of life. The spiritual life is a life of Christian discipline (worship, service, prayer, study, care, and concern for others) that is based upon thanksgiving for the blessings and gifts of God.

When the hope of deepening of the spiritual life is expressed, the question is often, "How can I draw closer, or feel closer, to God?" But it is not a question of God's coming closer to us— God is already present. How can I become more aware of and responsive to that presence? The answers are many and varied—

prayer, worship, study, personal meditation, use of the Bible and other resources, serving and loving. Perhaps one of the most important ways is to spend time and be in contact with those persons who demonstrate the kind of spiritual life you want to emulate.

To develop a spiritual life is to develop the Christian life. Eventually and ultimately, all we do as the followers of Christ is based upon the spiritual facts of the faith. Everything we do has its spiritual basis. The lowest menial task has its spirituality—that is, it is based upon God's love for us and our responses to it.

Additional Resource

Thomas Moore, *Care of the Soul: A Guide for Cultivating Depth and Sacredness in Everyday Life* (New York: HarperCollins, 1992).

NEVER TOO OLD TO LEARN

> *You shall love the Lord your God with all your heart, and with all your soul, and with all your strength, and with all your mind.*
>
> —*Luke 10:27*

GEORGE BUTTRICK, born in 1892, was known as the "Preacher of Preachers." He once said, "We must build church doors high enough so that people don't have to leave their heads outside."

Your church, believing that the Christian faith also involves the mind (are we not to love God with our minds?) and knowing that ours is also an intellectual faith, encourages you to use your mind, to learn, to ask questions, to seek new knowledge, to wonder about life.

Somehow the notion began, especially in churches that observe the rite of confirmation, that the age of junior high school signals an end to learning. Church school participation beyond the eighth or ninth grade is little, if any. In too many churches the total program of adult education consists of the four participants (all seventy years of age) in the Sunday Bible class!

Your church is encouraged to have an active adult education program: Bible study, current events, general discussion, and growth groups. Equally important is your participation. Perhaps you will have access to such topics for study as the following:

A Look at the Cults
The Dead Sea Scrolls
Death and Dying

Amos Speaks to the Twentieth Century
A Study of World Religions
Understanding the Roman Catholic Church
Christmas Customs
Introduction to Church Music
Comparing the New Bible Versions and Translations
Mark, the First Gospel
Understanding Christian Science, the Mormons, etc.

All these topics were included during the Sunday church school hour in one church's adult education program over a two-year span. That church was probably not much different from yours. You can do it too.

> *It's a great pity that things weren't so arranged that an empty head, like an empty stomach, wouldn't let its owner rest until something was put into it.*[18]

Every group meeting will prove to be fruitful ground. It is reported that even some official boards make an educational topic part of their agenda. What better place to begin than at the top!

Small groups are effective settings for learning—or for that matter, for support, for serving, for fellowship. Many of the fastest-growing churches build their programs around small groups in which each person is an important part and in which each person feels at home. One model, developed some years ago by Henry Tani (then a youth director of the United Church of Christ), was called the "Four S's"—eight to ten persons, meeting weekly at the group's choice of time and place, together for 3–4 months, working on an agenda of four S's:

Study—a topic of interest and growth
Service—a project that reached out and touched others
Skill—the group learned a skill
Social—they planned a social event for the group

ME—A COUNSELOR?

> *Bear one another's burdens.*
>
> *—Galatians 6:2*

Yes, and why not? Earlier in this book, reference was made to each member of the church being called to ministry, to service. This includes being concerned for other members, be they family, friends, and/or others.

We have great opportunities to be counselors. In daily living we encounter, almost routinely, any number of situations where a friendly ear can prove invaluable: sickness, death, loss of a job, family problems, difficult decisions, loneliness, frustration, fear. Some of these situations approach us so subtly that it is easy to miss them. Be alert; they are fields of ministry.

By and large, few persons want "advice"—even those who come looking for it. But most have a story to tell, a tale of woe, a disaster that is theirs—and they are looking for someone who will listen. Listening, then, becomes our field of ministry. Jesus was effective because he was so willing to listen. He invited persons to speak, to share their story. He gave them the time necessary.

> How long has he had this? (Mark 9:21)
>
> What do you want me to do for you? (Luke 18:41)
>
> What is your name? (Mark 5:9)

Your ministry, too, can be effective. You'll need "ears that hear," a concern for persons, willingness to use time and to be inconvenienced. This ministry requires all these.

Some suggested guidelines for this listening ministry are:

1. Be available and ready to give time.
2. Be an active listener. Ask for clarification. Repeat what you heard. Keep the story clearly in mind.
3. Look for nonverbal signs.[19] Tightly clenched fists will repudiate the words, "I am *not* angry." Be sensitive to facial expression (or lack of), posture, face color, hand and arm movements (or nonmovement). Each nonverbal conveys a message. Help the person put into words the feelings that are physically expressed.
4. Don't be shocked by what you hear. (At least don't outwardly indicate any shock.) Avoid pronouncing judgments, if at all possible.
5. Remember, you are hearing only one side of a story. Most stories have at least two sides.
6. You need not agree with all that is being said in order to indicate your loving care. Avoid taking sides. You might suggest that there be a mediator, a go-between.
7. Know your limitations. Don't take on more than you can handle. Admit when you feel inadequate for the situation. Be ready to refer to another listener, perhaps a professional. Feel free to consult professionals for assistance; most are quite willing to cooperate.
8. Respect confidentiality. The story that was related to you is a sacred trust and was intended for your ears alone.

It is encouraging to know that there is great therapeutic value in being able to speak with another person about a problem. In the telling of the story, many people are able to clarify their situation. It has been said that a problem properly clarified and identified is a problem already half-solved.

Welcome to the ministry of listening and caring.

YOU'RE A HOSPITAL CHAPLAIN

I was sick and you took care of me.
                                    —*Matthew 25:36b*

THIS section on being an effective hospital visitor is viewed from the patient's perspective. The normal hospital setting is assumed. Follow-up upon the patient's return home is also very important. The change from the busy hospital routine to the relative isolation of home can lead to depression and loneliness.

Thank you for coming. You have come from a world to which I plan to return—the sooner the better. You represent love and thoughtfulness. It is good to be remembered, to be important!

You remind me that I am a person with a name. Here I am sometimes referred to as "that gall bladder in 518–l." Your visit is a high point in my day. It is second only to my getting out.

To help make your visit a good experience, I am sharing these thoughts with you. Because of my stay in a hospital I know *my* visits will never again be the same.

When you visit, don't expect to be entertained. Some visitors leave feeling unhappy because I did not make them feel at home or keep conversation moving. Yes, this room is my home and I am the host/hostess, but not because I want it that way. I have a problem—I'm sick. Please don't look for me to be a gracious welcomer, even though I want to be, or expect me to be responsible for your comfort and enjoyment.

As you enter my room, be prepared for anything. Don't be visibly upset if you see a multitude of bottles, tubes, equipment. My appearance could shock you; don't let it show. Avoid the use of "encouraging" remarks such as, "You look awful!" I don't need that kind of encouragement.

You'll be here during visiting hours. The hours may be inconvenient, but they have been set for the good of the patient and not to suit visitors. Much of the work is done during off-hours. This is also a time for me to rest. Visitors can tire a patient. Therefore, although I am pleased to see you, I might also be happy when you leave. Be alert to signs of weariness or discomfort. Don't wear me out with conversation. If I'm yawning, restless, checking the time, thanking you for coming, these could be hints that our visit has run its course.

This *is* a hospital. Many seriously ill persons (surrounded by loved ones) are here. Boisterous talk is disturbing. Be sensitive to my roommate's condition. He/she might have received bad news today or might not be feeling well.

Avoid sitting on or bumping my bed. It and I have become very close—at times too close. We have become a unit. We are one. I can feel every bump and jar. But, if possible, shake my hand, give me a hug, a kiss; I need the reassurance found in such physical actions.

My life is literally in my physician's hands. I'm trying to trust the treatment. Don't question my doctor's qualifications. Avoid the temptation to diagnose my illness with statements such as, "Well, it certainly appears that you have what my Aunt Jane had, and *her* doctor said . . . ."

I would appreciate your not talking illnesses when we visit. The conversation of hospital visitors invariably includes a recounting of every illness anyone ever had and the gorier the better. I am weary of illness. Don't burden me with others' medical problems; mine is enough for the time being.

If we are going to talk doctors or illness or hospital care, allow me to take the lead, to give permission to do so. Some griping will be good for me. It is said that in the military, when there is no griping, morale is low. Let me spout off; you don't have to agree or enhance it. Let me set the agenda. It might be that I want you to be here, saying very little. Don't be embarrassed if I don't feel like conversing. Your presence has already been worthwhile.

It is not necessary that you know all the details of my illness or surgery. Please don't pry. I will share with you what I want to share. After all, you have come to see me and not a certain part of my anatomy. Some things will be apparent (a broken leg); some things can be rather private (hemorrhoids).

Be the bearer of good news. Share good things with me. Have a smile on your face. But don't be phony; be yourself, the person I know. I prefer honesty. Patients are *not* the last to know. We know more than given credit for. When we are seriously ill, we know it. We don't need visitors pretending all is well. Be alert, be sensitive. I will give you clues as to how honest I want you to be with me.

Check with my nurse before bringing me candy, fruit, and so on. Certain goodies might be restricted. Smoking is taboo. (Patients may be allowed to smoke in their rooms, but not visitors. Respiratory ailments are aggravated by smoke. The rooms are small, and remember what the surgeon general said.)

Looks like I've done all the talking. I'm glad you care; please come again. But before you leave, could we have prayer together?

Additional Resources

John E. Biegert, *Looking Up . . . While Lying Down* (Cleveland: The Pilgrim Press, 1979). A 24-page booklet of prayers, scripture, and meditations for hospitalized people. You may want to use it as part of your visit or leave it with the patient.

Joan E. Hemenway, *Holding On . . . While Letting Go* (Cleveland: The Pilgrim Press, 1985).

Geneva M. Butz, *Color Me Well: A Coloring/Prayer Book for Children* (Cleveland: The Pilgrim Press, 1986).

Harold S. Kushner, *When Bad Things Happen to Good People* (New York: Avon, 1981).

PLANNING FOR THOSE BIG EVENTS

> *Rejoice with those who rejoice, weep with those who weep.*
> —*Romans 12:15*

LAMENTING that some people only use the church now and then, someone coined the phrase, "The church is used for matching, hatching, and dispatching" (that is, weddings, baptisms, and funerals).

Yet weddings, funerals, and baptisms (and confirmation) are big events in the lives of those involved and in the life of the total church. To ensure that these "big" events are also meaningful and Christian, careful planning is necessary. Your church undoubtedly has guidelines and expectations for each of these events, but allow a few comments to be made concerning, not the mechanics of each, but some attitudes and ideals.

Baptism belongs in the presence of a worshiping congregation. Baptism—the reception of a person into the church—needs the presence of the church, for it also has the function of sponsor, of godparent. The welfare, spiritual and otherwise, of the newly baptized person is of prime concern to the church.

Except in the most unusual of circumstances, there is no reason for "private" or home baptisms. Baptism is an event that calls for the participation of the entire church because, after all, here one is entering the entire church.

Confirmation is not a "graduation" from the church but a "commencement" *into* the life of the church. The baptized person "agrees" (confirms) with the content and the badge of baptism. The church welcomes the person and, in many cases, confers certain privileges (for example, voting rights).

Weddings. A wedding service *is* a service of worship. In that respect, God is the center of attention. (Unfortunately, many wedding services see the bride and groom and not God as the center of attention. This is apparent in the choice of music, the fashion-parade entrance, the flash of cameras.) A carefully planned service not only accomplishes the purpose of joining two in marriage but also worships God as the center of life. Allow sufficient time for thorough consultation with your pastor. Don't wait until two weeks before the wedding to see if the "preacher" is available.

Funerals. More thought needs to be given to church funerals. Funeral homes for many are places of death whereas the church building speaks of Christmas hymns, Easter, children, the gospel, life, and hope. Here in the meetinghouse are symbols that are meaningful—symbols of the presence and the love of God. Closed caskets are suggested for the service, regardless of location. An open casket remains the center of focus; a closed casket enables the elements of worship—the symbols, the spoken and sung word—to do their healing work.

Some congregations use their meetinghouses for both—visitation and the service. Depending upon such variables as parking, handicapped accessibility, and space, many persons prefer the warm, friendly, familiar surroundings of their church building.

Visitation is enhanced with the presence of cookies and coffee provided by some group or circle.

Anniversaries and Birthdays. A happy characteristic of a congregation is that it is composed of persons who "rejoice with those who rejoice." Birthdays and anniversaries are times for rejoicing (in spite of the aches and pains of advancing age). Providing flowers for the Sunday worship service is one vehicle used to invite others to join in your joy.

Some anniversaries that need celebrating and that often escape our notice are the age of the congregation (year of founding), significant events in the life of that congregation, and pastoral anniversaries (year of service or ordination). One congregation placed roses on the communion table each year on the anniversary of its pastor's arrival (the number of roses denoting the years of service).

Surprise celebrations and those that are planned for the outdoors are always enjoyable and add a dimension of warmth often missing in the rush of modern living.

WHEN SOMEONE DIES

> *When this perishable body puts on imperishability, and this mortal body puts on immortality, then the saying that is written will be fulfilled: "Death has been swallowed up in victory."*
>
> *—1 Corinthians 15:54*

"FRIENDS may call tomorrow from two to nine P.M."

That sentence signals the beginning of a service opportunity for you as a member of the church. A friend, acquaintance, fellow member, or loved one has died, and you'll be visiting the family at the funeral home or at church. You can go to "get it over with," to pay your respects, or you can visit as a concerned, caring friend and a Christian minister.

It is hoped you will go as the latter. To help you be an effective visitor and minister, it will help to keep the following in mind:

Be aware of your feelings about death and suffering. You will be unable to assist others in accepting the reality of death if you deny it. Expressions such as "He's sleeping" or "He's passed away" or "She's gone to be with her maker" are often ways of avoiding the finality of death.

Know the purpose of your visit. You will be little help if you simply follow the socially accepted custom of paying respects. On the other hand, a visit with the intent of giving love and of sharing sorrow will be a meaningful one.

Greet the mourners in some physical manner—a handshake, a hug, a kiss. Many mourners, looking back on the funeral home vigil, report that they remembered little of what was said, but they did recall those who were present, especially those who *did* something (hug, kiss, cry). If there is some hesitation of recognition, introduce yourself. This is no time for a "Guess Who?" game.

Let the mourners do the talking. Don't be afraid of silence. Listen to what they want to talk about. Don't pry; the details might be none of your business.

Be concerned for the mourners. Care for their physical well-being.

Avoid the well-intentioned but often meaningless cliches. ("She looks nice." "Was it an easy death?" "My, what pretty flowers!" "Don't cry, he is better off now.")

Allow tears to flow (yours and theirs). Men are advised that there is no law against male tears. Tears are not a sign of weakness but of humanity.

Offer whatever help you can. Follow through, of course.

As you leave, know that your ministry has only begun. Your love, concern, and presence will be needed in the days, weeks, and months to come. Don't wait to be called. A general rule is that the time mourners are avoiding people is when they most need to be around supportive persons. Don't be pushy, but take the initiative.

Additional Resources

There are many helpful books available on the subjects of death and dying. You can perform a vital and needed ministry in assisting persons through this common experience of life.

Four booklets published by The Pilgrim Press, Cleveland, as part of the "Looking Up Series": John E. Biegert, *When Death Has Touched Your Life*, 1981, and *My Loved One Is Dying*, 1980; Lois A. Bloom, *Mourning After Suicide*, 1986; Doris Stickney, *Water Bugs and Dragonflies*, 1982 (a story for young children about death).

Leslie D. Weatherhead, *The Will of God* (Nashville: Abingdon, 1980). A classic, first published in 1944.

Granger Westberg, *Good Grief* (Philadelphia: Fortress Press, 1971).

THOSE INVISIBLE MEMBERS

> *I was a stranger and you welcomed me. . . . I was in prison and you visited me.*
>
> —*Matthew 25:35–36*

By now you've probably seen most of the active members of your congregation in worship and in other settings. You don't know all their names, but you recognize their faces.

There are other members you will not see. Most of them have long records of loving service in the church. Most of them contribute to the financial support of the church. They are "present" in the worship service but are unseen. I refer to those who are homebound. Infirmity, old age, lack of transportation, and other problems have combined to confine them to wheelchairs, nursing homes, beds, or one room. Unlike many ambulatory members who could participate but don't, these persons want to participate but cannot.

Homebound members will remain unseen and unknown to you unless you visit them. And until you meet them, *you* will remain unknown to them and be only a name on a membership roll.

One of the most significant actions of the early church, the selection of deacons (Acts 6:1–7), took place out of a concern for such as these.

A significant experience awaits you—and someone who is homebound—should you decide to transform an unseen member (a stranger) into a loving friend. Here's one way to go about it.

1. *Secure the name* of a homebound member from your pastor or the church office. Seek pertinent information about the

person. Your congregation might have an established group for this purpose—offer your service.

2. *Make an appointment to visit.* Call ahead, if possible, and introduce yourself as a visitor from "our church." Set up a mutually agreeable time. If the person is in a hospital or nursing home, visiting hours will determine the time.

3. *Know why you are visiting.* Visit as a member of the family—the church—seeking to share life with a fellow member. You will receive a great deal of satisfaction, and as others have discovered, you'll probably receive more than you give. Share good news—news of the church, news of their friends.

4. *Offer help within your capability.* If you offer assistance in any form or ask if there is anything you can do, be certain to offer only what you can deliver. Once you have committed yourself to a course of action, know that you are being trusted to come through. If you promise to return on a certain day, be there on that day; you will be expected.

5. *Between visits,* phone calls, cards, and other little remembrances are always cherished and often become the high points of a day.

6. *Be prepared for a grand and glorious feeling!*

7. *Seek training* on how to be an effective homebound caller. If none is available, encourage the establishment of a training group.

Your concern for homebound members will lead you to ask some searching questions, chief among them being, "How open and accessible is our church building (and program) to those with a physical and/or mental disability?" Are some members forced to drop out because of inaccessibility? What about members with brain injuries, those who are deaf or blind, or members in wheelchairs? What are we doing for these and many others?

There is an abundance of materials on "accessibility" available from denominational and governmental sources. Much of it will be helpful in identifying and helping to meet the needs of what might be termed "invisible" disabilities (lung and heart ailments, arthritic conditions, sight and hearing problems).

YOU'RE AN EVANGELIST, REACHING OUT TO OTHERS

> *And Jesus said to them, "Follow me, and I will make you fish for people."*
>
> —*Matthew 4:19*

THE Christian faith is not a religion. Surprised? You shouldn't be, especially if you agree with one definition of religion as an "attempt to find God." The reverse is true for Christians. We believe that God has reached out to us. (See Luke 19:10.)

We, the church, began by God's reaching out to us, seeking us, and thereby setting the pattern by which the church was to live and grow. Recall the words of the Great Commission: "Go into all the world" (Matthew 28:19–20).

For almost two thousand years the church has lived and grown as God continues to reach out through the members of the church, God's tools, God's instruments of outreach. The church has grown because church members shared a story and invited others to join them in this family of Christ.

We have a story to tell: the good news (evangel). (Evangelism can be defined as good news-ism.) Upon hearing the word *evangelism* certain images tend to come to mind: tent meetings, TV-radio preaching, crusades, revivals, a Jehovah's Witness at your door. Let us move from these narrow uses back to the broadest understandings of evangelism.

A classic definition of evangelism has been "one beggar telling another beggar where to find bread."

Some contend that the "getting of new members" is the job of the pastor or of the evangelism committee. Why did *you* join?

Because of the pastor, a committee, or was there some other compelling reason?

There have been many studies done on the influences leading persons to join the church. One of these studies on influences is listed below:[20]

Walked in off the street	3–8%
Attracted by some church program	4–10%
Drawn by the pastor	10–20%
Result of special church visitation	10–25%
Through the church school	3–6%
Brought by relative or friend	60–90%

The last item is in italics for good reason. Although the other items of the study are essential to the ongoing work of the church, *the value of each member as an evangelist is undeniable.* If a congregation is to grow, it is assumed that the pastor will play a key role. Equally important, perhaps more so, is the role that each member has. (Who can argue with the figures?)

OK, you're convinced. You're an evangelist. The question now is how does one go about doing the job? Lyle E. Schaller, a consultant with the Yokefellow Institute in Richmond, Indiana, has listed "Twelve Ways to Keep People from Joining Your Church." Here are some of them:

1. Don't invite them.
2. Have a sanctuary seating six hundred persons not even one third filled.
3. Think of your church as small and insignificant.
4. Plan for buildings, not for persons.
5. Cut back on the number of groups and programs.

6. Trust your church building to do the attracting.
7. Offer newcomers three choices:
    a. Take what we offer.
    b. Stay home.
    c. Go somewhere else.[21]

Apparently, part of doing the work of evangelizing is to reverse these ways of keeping persons away. Here are some additional points to consider.

How does one go about being an evangelist? Intentionally so. Potential members receive a first impression of a church through its worship service. It is important that the whole church be found in worship. The Sunday you miss might be the Sunday you were most needed to smile, to love, to care, to greet. Empty pews carry strong, negative messages. Warmth and friendliness are two assets you bring to worship. You might ask for names and addresses of visitors and offer to follow up with a personal visit. Invite nonchurch friends and relatives to worship with you.

Unintentionally so. Encourage a warm, caring spirit within your congregation. Seek to deepen your commitment, participation, and faith. Clearly, it is those churches that care, that genuinely love, that are the growing, vital churches.

Purify your motives. If new members are sought only to balance the budget or to reduce the load on present members or to replace tired members, your efforts will produce little results. Ours is a missionary faith. That is, the news is so good, so wonderful that we cannot contain it; it must be shared. Good things have happened to us. In the spirit of love we want them to happen to others, also.

Be alert and responsive to the needs of those who are searching. Those with young children will be concerned for good child care. The nursery and those staffing it are often factors that determine whether visitors return. Is there somewhere new persons can "plug in"? A place for them to belong? Whether we like it or not, there is present a "shopper's mentality." What do you have to offer me? What worked with one generation might not work with another. There are differing expectations. Consider parking: the "older" generation asked, "What's a parking lot?" The "middle" generation exclaimed, "Thank goodness, I found a parking space!" The "younger" set expectantly inquires, "Where is your parking lot?"

The growing, attracting church has managed with a creative approach to reach out to all persons without sacrificing the ideals and dignity of the church and its savior, Jesus Christ.

NOTE: A major concern in the church is what to do with those members who drop out, the no-shows, the disgruntled. One approach, the hard-nosed, is to ignore them for at least a few years, after which they are erased from membership. Another is to place them on a list of inactive members and hope for the "miracle" that will bring them back. Still a third is the one Jesus used: leave the ninety-nine who are safe and secure and go out to search actively for that one who is "lost" (Luke 15:3–7). Perhaps you have heard of the 5 C's of evangelism:

Contact (determine who are the prospects)

Cultivate them, tell them of the church and its savior

Commitment is sought

Churchmanship is taught

Conservation—keeping and involving the new
member once he or she has joined

At this point we are speaking of *conservation,* seeking to keep members from dropping out. The church is missing the point if it does not work at least as diligently to conserve its members as it does to seek new ones.

MEET THE TATER FAMILY[22]

> *Beloved, do not believe every spirit, but test the spirits to see whether they are from God; for many false prophets have gone out into the world.*
>
> —*1 John 4:1*

CHECK your congregation's membership directory. Look under the T's. Any Taters listed? Chances are there are none, but chances are you will "find" them under the A's, B's, and all the way through to the Z's. (This is meant to be tongue-in-cheek, for the Taters serve us by identifying all those stereotypes of members we know so well.)

As you meet the Taters, perhaps you will recognize a similarity to a member of your church. But beware of any temptation to condemn. One or more of the Taters could be you. Remember what happened to King David and the prophet Nathan? (See 2 Samuel 12:1–7.)

> Hear the words
> Not so humorous
> Of the "Tater"
> Much too numerous:
>
> "Spec-Tater is my name.
> Sittin' n' watchin's my game.
> And if work you dare mention,
> I'll be off to some convention!"

The fact of the matter is, we are all members of the Tater family: at times negative, at times positive. As in the parable of the four soils (Mark 4:3–8), we can be one or more of the soils Jesus speaks about. (Our goal, of course, is to become the "soil" that produces a good harvest. We will find some Taters that appeal while others will appall. Having said this, it's time to meet the family.)

Vege-Tater is quite content to sit and sit and sit, quite content to let others do the work. *Vege* will speak up when things don't work out too well but will accept none of the responsibility for how things are. And then there's *Dic-Tater,* who's always ready to take over. Just ask *Dic-Tater* and you'll be told what to do. (Often you don't even have to ask!) *Ampu-Tater* will effectively cut down, take apart, and tear to shreds people and projects. Closely related, *Devas-Tater* leaves a wake of human debris. *Facili-Tater,* a vivid contrast to these latter two, will get the project "off the ground" and working. Then there are two who keep track of everything, making sure they do no more than anyone else. They are quick to ask and answer the question, "What did we do last year?" Their names are *Anno-Tater* and *Compu-Tater.*

> *Therefore, be imitators of God, as beloved children.*
> —*Ephesians 5:1*

> Now this advice is sound:
> Can there by any greater?
> It's become the motto of
> Our good friend *Imi-Tater.*

Prepare to meet some real troublemakers. As you know, there is "good" trouble and "bad" trouble, depending upon your perspective. Sometimes these two stir up interest and the result is forward movement; sometimes they just stir up! Introducing: *Irri-Tater* and cousin *Agi-Tater!* Other members of the family move more cautiously: "We've never done it *that* way!" they warn. Caution, at times, is a virtue, but if *Hesi-Tater* prevailed all the time, nothing would happen. At that moment, you need help! So call upon *Levi-Tater* to raise your concern in prayer.

> *You shall love the Lord your God with all your heart, and with all your soul, and with all your strength, and with all your mind. (Luke 10:27)*

Some say, "Never wonder."
Some say, "Never ask."
Some say, "Ask no questions;
Blind faith only is our task."

Now workers are needed
And action to be commended.
"But," reminds *Medi-Tater,*
"Use your mind as God commanded."

There is one more Tater, who is not really of the immediate family. (This one's a poor speller.) This Tater will encourage you to loaf in your church membership. Take it easy. No need to rush or to be excited and enthused about Christ's church. Put things off. (May this breed decrease!) Say goodbye to *Procrasti-Tater.*

WHEN CONTROVERSY ERUPTS

> *... let us all speak the truth to our neighbors, for we are members of one another. Be angry but do not sin; do not let the sun go down on your anger, and do not make room for the devil.*
>
> *—Ephesians 4:25–27*

"What a terrible disgrace," complained the letter to the editor, "allowing the flag over the veterans' section of the cemetery to become so tattered!" Written by a member of the local veterans' organization, the letter proceeded to condemn the cemetery management for its failure to keep a crisp, new flag flying.

SHORTLY thereafter appeared the cemetery superintendent's reply: it seems that it was the responsibility of the local veterans' group to provide the flag used in that section.

Following publication of the reply, there were some red faces around town, to say nothing of hurt feelings and much embarrassment. All of that could have been avoided if one upset veteran had made one phone call to one cemetery superintendent.

How does this apply to controversy in the church? Only to suggest that many a disagreement, many a controversy, can be avoided or settled quickly with an honest gathering of facts. Contact those closest to the problem or those involved or those who have pertinent information. Often a call to the church office, an officer, or the pastor will clear up a rumor or a misconception.

The church—composed of human beings, sinners, if you will—can expect times of difficulty from both within and without. There will always be tension between the church and the world, between God's way and other ways. Jesus recognized this when he said, "In the world you have tribulation" (John 16:33). The very nature of the gospel is such that it confronts the world and its greed, selfishness, self-centeredness. In fact, the church, when it is being *the* church in the world, will be embroiled continually in controversy.

What happens, however, when member disagrees with member or faction with faction? How do we deal with those nasty church fights that often result in *church flight?*

We need to begin with the recognition that we are the people of God, that we together stand under the judgment of God. "All have sinned, all have gone astray." Standing, then, in need of God's love and forgiveness, we approach one another in the same spirit of love. (You can be angry with those you love, but love sets the ground rules for disagreements. For example, love reminds us that the opponent is a fellow member of the family, not some horrible foe, animal, monster.)

Love enables us to center upon issues and not personalities. We are so easily hurt. We take everything personally. We forget that it is possible to disagree, yet to love. (It is seen often in legislative bodies that bitter foes "on the floor" are actually close, personal friends.)

Love enables us to trust another, even in disagreement. Frequently issues arise that permit conflicting views with justification for each. Rather than insisting that all agree, it is possible to allow those who support a cause to do so while the rest choose not to. (For example, Habitat for Humanity will interest some, whereas others might be drawn to a project for neighborhood drug awareness. Both can co-exist in the same fellowship.)

One congregation faced with a divisive vote concerning homosexuality averted much of the "fire" by first appointing a task force composed of all sides of the issue to study the topic and then report back with a recommendation. Though not all agreed with the final outcome, all agreed that it is possible to disagree and remain members of the One Body of Christ.

Matthew 18:15ff touches upon settling differences. The procedure outlined is: (1) Deal with difficulties person to person. (2) If the issue cannot be dealt with solely by the parties, seek a few trusted persons to help. (3) If that does not work, then it becomes a concern of the entire congregation. (The embarrassment of the cemetery-flag letter could have been avoided if this procedure had been followed.)

At times the assistance of an outsider is invaluable for sorting out the issue from that which is clouding it. Such a resource person might be a denominational staff person, regional church and ministry committee, or someone mutually acceptable to all the parties.

The beneficial aspects of controversies is that they pinpoint areas needing work. Once that work is completed, the congregation will be free to move ahead in the work and service of Christ in a more united and committed way. (The best part of a marital disagreement is making up afterwards. Could that apply also to the family called "church"?)

A word about anger. Anger is not wrong, it is one feeling among the dozens we experience. The rightness or wrongness of anger is what we do with it or allow it to do with us. There is a place for righteous anger; there is not a place for destructive anger. Some anger is displaced anger, that is, anger that belongs to one person or situation is expressed in another. (The boss chews me out, so I come home and kick the dog.) Much criticism and hard feelings come out of this scenario in the church. In the extreme, persons who are angry with God take it out on the church or on particular church members—especially the leadership of the church.

When anger is directed toward you, it is helpful to ask: (1) Do I deserve the anger? (2) How much of this anger will I keep and how much will I let pass through? (3) How can I help to defuse it? (4) With whom and what is this person really angry?

Additional Resources

Les Carter and Frank Minirth, *The Anger Workbook* (Nashville: Thomas Nelson, 1993).

Charles H. Cosgrove and Dennis Hatfield, *Church Conflict: The Hidden Systems Behind the Fights* (Nashville: Abingdon, 1994).

NO ONE APPRECIATES ME! I QUIT!

> *So you also, when you have done all that you were ordered to do, say, "We are worthless slaves; we have done only what we ought to have done!"*
>
> *—Luke 17:10*

At one time or another most of us in the church have grumbled, "No one appreciates me!" We have felt that our work and efforts are unnoticed and unappreciated.

It is hoped we will not drop out of the church, as did the woman whose pickles were not used at the annual church dinner.

It is good to be appreciated, to be noticed. There is nothing wrong with making appreciation known; it is done too seldom. Perhaps others feel as we do. When *they* say, "No one appreciates me!" could it be that their "no one" is *me*?

Feelings of lack of appreciation raise key questions:

1. Did I join the church to be appreciated?
2. What is my reason for serving? To gain glory for me?
3. Why am I a Christian? To win some kind of medal?

This would be a good time to read Matthew 5:16, 25:31–45, and Luke 17:7–10. Having read these, do you still feel unappreciated? Do you suppose Jesus could have felt that way on Good Friday?

"Unappreciated" usually means "unthanked." "No one has thanked me," I complain. But we might have it twisted. The Christian life is not a life of *expecting* or *receiving* thanks. Rather it is one of *giving thanks*. It is a style of life in which God is thanked for the gifts of love, salvation, meaning, and purpose for life.

The point is that we can never fully thank (repay) God for the above gifts. (And if you think *you're* unappreciated, check with God!)

Thanksgiving means *thanks-living*. (God saved Israel from slavery under Egypt by sending Moses and deliverance. God loved them. Israel, in effect, at Sinai asked, "How can we thank God?" The reply came, "By living in such a manner," and the Ten Commandments were given.)

The most important words of praise will come from God: "Well done, good and faithful servant." With this in mind, our motto becomes, "Do good, and forget about it!"

This is not to suggest that we never honor or praise persons. It is a wonderful thing for the church to recognize special achievements, anniversaries of service, retirements, long service rendered. It can be seen that God expresses thanks through human thanks. The only point being made is that the best service is rendered, not from hope of reward, but from the basis of thanksgiving.

THE CHURCH BEYOND
THE FRONT DOORS

> *For we hear that some of you are living in idleness, mere busybodies, not doing any work.*
>
> *—2 Thessalonians 3:11*

As an active member of the congregation you will be involved in the life of that fellowship, in the many and varied callings and tasks needed to make yours a viable fellowship. The church can only be and do what its members want it to.

But the church is operative in spheres other than the local parish. There are local and wider-area councils of churches. Your denomination has several levels of work: local, regional, state, national, and international. Those willing to become involved outside of the local "four walls" will find meaningful work and experiences.

There are community projects and causes that need the support and involvement of church members: Red Cross, cancer foundations, FISH, hospital auxiliaries, United Way, various youth organizations (such as the YMCA and YWCA), and many more excellent causes.

Being a member of the church—a Christian, a follower of the Way of Christ—is a twenty-four-hours-a-day calling. We seek to live what we believe. We carry our beliefs into every part of our daily activity.

Wherever you serve you will be a message of love, care, and concern: the hallmarks of the church.

Recall the "badge" of baptism—how we are called to wear that badge always. It is an awesome privilege and responsibility.

Whatever I do, whatever I say—there is the church! Wherever I am—at home, at work, in school, in recreation—Wherever I spend time—there is the church (in me!).

JUST IN CASE YOU MISSED IT . . .

> *But the angel said to them, "Do not be afraid; for see—I am bringing you good news of great joy for all the people: to you is born this day in the city of David a Savior, who is the Messiah, the Lord."*
>
> *—Luke 2:10–11*

God created the world and saw that it was good. God created humankind and desired its love and companionship. God did not force love and companionship upon the creation but gave it a choice to love or reject. Unfortunately, the created wanted to be the creator. Humankind attempted to play God and turned its worship away from God and toward itself. The created tried (tries) to be the center of life rather than the recipient of Life. And that's what sin is all about!

Yet God loved the creation, humankind. Not content to allow humankind to destroy itself, God began to reach out, to seek for, to call back to the Godself the fallen creation. The Old Testament is filled with examples of the efforts of God to restore communication, to create a special fellowship.

The work of God to save, restore, and recreate humankind reaches its climax in the New Testament accounts of the Son, the Savior, Jesus the Christ. Through the life, death, and resurrection of the Son, God accepts humankind as forgiven, redeemed, and restored. Now the question is, how will God convey that message to the creation?

When Jesus departed from this earth, he left no written words, no possessions to speak of, nothing of apparent value—but he did leave followers to carry on his work of redemption and salvation. Through the power of the Holy Spirit, he left behind the church!

You, when together with others, are that church.

You, when by yourself, are that church.

You are the church!

Your mission is that of God the Creator, to love!

Your mission is to introduce others to the God who created us, and who loves us, and who wants us to enjoy Life.

> I am the church!
> You are the church!
> We are the church together!
> All who follow Jesus,
> all around the world!
> Yes, we're the church together.[23]

AND NOW . . .

What is *my* understanding of the church?

What do I believe?

Notes

1. A. M. Hunter, *A Pattern for Life* (Philadelphia: Westminster Press, 1953).
2. See the Library of Christian Classics, vol. 1, Early Christian Fathers (Philadelphia: Westminster Press, 1953), 161–79.
3. Oliver Powell, *Household of Power* (New York: The Pilgrim Press, 1962), 61–62.
4. Richard Avery and Donald Marsh, *We Are the Church* (Carol Stream, Ill.: Hope Publishing, 1972). Used by permission.
5. Roger Lincoln Shinn and Daniel Day Williams, *We Believe: An Interpretation of the United Church Statement of Faith* (New York: United Church Press, 1966), 98.
6. Roland H. Bainton, *The Age of the Reformation* (New York: Van Nostrand Reinhold, 1956).
7. Winfred E. Garrison, *A Protestant Manifesto* (Nashville: Abingdon Press, 1952), 48.
8. Ibid., 22ff.
9. Approved by the UCC Executive Council, October 31, 1981, for use in 1982, the twenty-fifth anniversary year of the United Church of Christ.
10. A. Gordon Nasby, ed., *One Thousand and Forty-One Sermon Illustrations, Ideas, and Expositions: Treasury of the Christian World* (New York: Harper and Row, 1953), 266.
11. Evangelical and Reformed Church, *Book of Worship* (Cleveland: Central Publishing House, 1947), 65.
12. Doug Meeks, *God the Economist* (Minneapolis: Fortress Press, 1989), 76.
13. *The Heidelberg Catechism*, 400th anniversary edition, 1563–1963, trans. Allen O. Miller and M. Eugene Osterhaven (New York: United Church Press, 1962), 9.

14. "The Order of Ordination to the Ministry," *Services of the Church*, no. 6 (New York: United Church Press, 1969), 3.
15. Ernest T. Campbell, "They Also Serve Who Lead," *Princeton Seminary Bulletin*, 1978, 3ff (commencement address).
16. Ibid.
17. Evangelical and Reformed Church, *Book of Worship* (Cleveland: Central Publishing House, 1947), 321f.
18. Miller Olin, *Ladies Home Journal*, reprinted in *Christian Leader's Golden Treasury*, ed. Maxwell Droke (New York: Grosset and Dunlap, 1955), 168.
19. Julius Fast, *Body Language* (New York: Pocket Books, 1971).
20. Lyle E. Schaller, "Evaluating the Potential for Growth," *The Christian Ministry*, January 1979, 5.
21. Lyle E. Schaller, *Assimilating New Members*, Creative Leadership Series (Nashville: Abingdon, 1978), 51ff.
22. This treatment of the Tater family is from an idea presented in a 1962 stewardship workshop by the Rev. Raymond Ley, then pastor of Zion United Church of Christ, Milwaukee.
23. Richard Avery and Donald Marsh, *We Are the Church* (Carol Stream, Ill.: Hope Publishing, 1972). Used by permission.